WORK FUR HIRE

TIPS, STORIES, & ACTIVITIES TO GET YOUR PAW IN THE DOOR

———————

Written and Edited By

Steven Hirsch, PhD

WORK FUR HIRE
Copyright © 2024 by Steven Hirsch, PhD

Cover art by Ben Geldenhuys
In-book illustrations by Nestor Antonio Martinez Ortega

All rights reserved. No part of this book may be reproduced or transmitted in any form or by any means without written permission from the author.

ISBN: 979-8-218-98784-8

Publisher –
Scribes Unlimited Press
2997 Keswick Rd
Cleveland OH 44120
info@scribesunlimited.com

DEDICATION

This book is dedicated to:

- Rama el Ligre for inspiring me to give back to a community by doing what I do best.

- Gre7g Luterman for showing me that writing a book was possible.

- The 61 companies that rejected my job applications in 2022. These experiences challenged me to think of job applications and hiring in a different way.

DISCLAIMER

The purpose of this book is to provide general guidance for individuals who are looking for employment. The advice contained in this book may not be applicable or appropriate for every job or industries. Careful consideration must be exercised when applying information from this book to inform a job search.

This book does not convey legal guidance. Guidance on legal matters should be directed to legal professionals who practice employment law within your jurisdiction.

The tips and end of chapter activities were written for individuals seeking employment within the United States of America. Refer to other resources for hiring practices in job markets outside the United States.

This is a work of fiction. Names, characters, businesses, places, events, locales, and incidents are either the products of the respective author's imagination or used in a fictitious manner. Any resemblance to actual persons, living or dead, or actual events is purely coincidental.

TABLE OF CONTENTS

FOREWORD

It was the summer of 2009. I had just graduated with a degree in Psychology from Boston University and was looking for a job. The housing market had crashed; they were calling it the worst job market since the Depression (little did we know what the COVID-19 Pandemic would bring…), and my Plan A jobs had vanished. I had been working seasonally at Philmont, a National Boy Scout summer camp in northern New Mexico, and tried networking with every adult who came through camp (which were hundreds). Nothing came from it, and Plan B fizzled.

I completed some pre-employment assessments and stepped out of camp with an approval letter to work for the Boy Scouts of America. This meant I could work for a local Scouting Council. I just needed to find a Council that was hiring. I went back to Phoenix, Arizona, where I was born and raised, and cooked up Plan C: a road trip through the West Coast, stopping at every Scouting Council along the way to ask for a job. With the family truck, a list of extended family who lived along I-5, and the cash from my summer job in hand, I hit the road. It took a month and driving all the way to Seattle to find a job.

For the next five years I worked as a District Executive with the Boy Scouts. I learned a lot about volunteer management, fundraising, and collaborating with a community while working for the Scouts, but I also discovered that I did not have the stomach for many of the situations that come up in counseling psychology (e.g., depression, anxiety). I had a blast working the volunteer politics and identifying who was the best for different volunteer roles. At that point I found out about Industrial Organizational (IO) Psychology. Think of it as the psychology of people at work, especially for measuring job relevant knowledge and skills during a hiring process. I applied to IO programs, got accepted, and left Scouting for graduate school.

Thirteen years after the West Coast road trip I found myself back in an awful job market. This time I had a PhD in IO Psychology from Central Michigan University, had relevant work experience building knowledge and skills assessments, and had a job as an external consultant with clients spanning many industries. Still, the job market was even worse than before (2022, COVID-19 Pandemic). The biggest difference from the summer of 2009 was I thoroughly understood the hiring game. I set out on a yearlong job search using everything I had learned from my schooling, research, and professional experience. Eventually my situation at work changed and the job search was called off, but I had developed so many tools and processes to help in my job search that it felt like a shame to put them aside to gather dust.

This book took inspiration from two places. First, my 2022 job search brought about insights about hiring that I have not seen mentioned in other job searching materials. It seemed natural to share my expertise and experiences with others who were embarking on a job search. Second, all the job search advice that I found had the same framing: some member of the majority wearing a suit or business casual describing "how to succeed" with business-sounding stories that lacked sincerity. The remedy for this tired framework was to build a book in a way that was the polar opposite of this "corporate training video" approach.

What you will find in this book is a collection of short stories about animal people (e.g., cartoon characters, anthropomorphic) who are in the throes of finding work. I hope that you find each story to be entertaining with how it discusses each tip, insightful with the information it provides, and sincere in representing our human experience with finding work.

INTRODUCTION

Hi! My name is Edwin and I am a job coach. A job coach is someone who prepares you for the job market. Although other counselors focus just on preparing for interviewing or crafting an appealing resume, a job coach helps with offering behind-the-scenes information about how hiring works, trends within the labor market, and insight into what happens within different trades. My goal is to share with you as much as I can so you are prepared for landing your dream job.

I am a hare, a black-tailed jackrabbit to be specific. Instead of just telling you how to go about your job search, I have collected several stories about animal people, like me, who have come across hardship while pursuing work. Each story was written by a different author, though some contributed multiple stories. Their information is included at the end of the book. Look them up if you enjoy their writing!

Each chapter of this collection is structured in the following way: The chapter title is the absolute shortest summary of the intended piece of advice. After that is a formal explanation of the message for the chapter. These are intended to set the mood, to point to something to keep in mind while you read the story. The stories range in genre, but they are all related to some step in the job searching process. Following each story are key takeaways, which are more in-depth information about the chapter's message. At the end of each chapter there is an activity to help you apply what was learned. These are either exercises (something to do) or reflections (something to think about). Lastly, some chapters conclude with a reality check. These are to point out parts of the story that wandered too far from realistic hiring situations.

The collection loosely follows the steps to getting a job, from looking for a job and networking, to resume building and interview preparation, to negotiating for better pay and other benefits. Every job search is different, so do not be surprised if your employment journey follows a different order than what is outlined in this collection. Keep in mind these stories were written broadly, intending to be relevant to a large number of jobs and industries. If there are specifics to the job, trade, or profession you are pursuing, then absolutely follow the norms for that industry.

You will get the most from this collection if you engage in its stories and activities. You do not have to do everything; I am sure there is something that is irrelevant to your job search. Regardless, you should give the activities a try. You never know what you may learn from the experience.

Lastly, let's be honest: the job searching process is time consuming, can be expensive, and is often demoralizing. I and the contributing authors will do our best to entertain, inform, and prepare you for your job search.

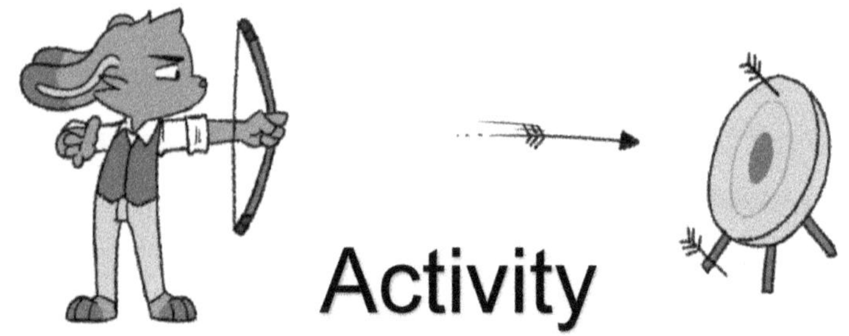

Creating a TO-DO list

This activity is intended to be ongoing as you read through this book. Take note of helpful takeaways, outcomes of end-of-chapter exercises, and any other information relevant to your situation. This may include tasks like creating a new professional-sounding email address, building a resume, or figuring out how to respond to common interview questions. Let's incorporate what was learned into your job search by creating a TO-DO list.

Exercise:
1. Begin reading and engaging with this book.

2. Take out a sheet of paper [yes, a physical sheet of paper].

3. Make a checklist of what you need for your job search based on what you have learned from the chapters of this book. List each item with a little box

you can check off once the item is completed. Make sure there is plenty of open space at the bottom of your paper.

4. Find a space that you often look at. This could be on the wall behind your computer monitor, refrigerator door, bathroom mirror, on your door leading outside, etc. Place the checklist there.

5. Start working through your checklist. Cross off items that you have completed and add new to-do items when needed.

6. Create a new checklist after your current sheet is completed or it has become too messy to understand.

CONGRATULATIONS! You have taken key steps in pursuing a job: creating a list of what needs to get done, setting up a reminder for what needs to get done, and establishing a method for tracking your progress.

CHAPTER ONE:
SEARCH SMARTER WITH BOOLEAN OPERATORS AND SEARCH FILTERS

Make the job board's search function do as much of the work as possible. Boolean search operators and search filters define keywords that the search engine uses to find applicable job postings and screens out what is irrelevant. Look online for guides on writing Boolean search operators for the job board(s) you are using. The goal is to minimize the junk job postings you must manually review.

Intense Search by Franklin T. Davis

Kris, a young ostrich in his last semester at university, sat at his desk in his dorm room. Many browser tabs were open on his laptop screen, and he could hear the fan humming quietly, trying to cool the CPU. Most tabs were different search engines that led to various job listings. However, Kris quickly became frustrated with how he had been spending nearly two hours browsing the posted openings.

"Gah! This is such a pain in my tailfeathers!" The irritated ostrich finally snapped as he pushed back in his seat. No sooner had he stood from his desk to get a water bottle from the mini-fridge than the hallway door opened, and his roommate, Wayne, entered.

"Jeez, I can hear you down the hall. What's wrong with you now? I mean, aside from the obvious?" The two had been friends since middle school, so the nonchalant wolf's banter elicited an amused snort from his feathered roommate.

"Oh, hey, man. Nothing's wrong, just lookin' online for some places to apply to," Kris replied.

"Told you that you shoulda started sooner," Wayne replied with a snarky grin and rifled through a dresser to pull out a fresh set of clothes.

The ostrich threw his winged hands up in exasperation. "I was busy!"

"Suuure…" came the snide comment.

Kris sat down at his desk again and noticed the laptop had hibernated. Frustrated, he restarted the machine and waited. He watched his wolf friend sort through more clothes, particularly a formal sweater and tie. "Hey, didn't you wear that when we went to dinner to celebrate your job offer a few weeks ago?"

Wayne looked at it and grinned. "Yeah, I did."

"Two weeks. How'd you find a position so quickly? All I've done is sift through millions of job postings, and I've gotten nowhere."

"What do you mean? Has it really taken that long for you?" The wolf approached the desk and looked at his laptop as it flashed back to life, revealing rows of job headings.

"Yeah, man! All these openings demand anywhere between two and sixteen years of workplace experience!"

The wolf chuffed. "You're exaggerating a bit with that sixteen years, aren't you?"

Kris shook his head and pointed to the laptop screen. "Could you just help me out over here? Don't make me beg."

"Fine, whatever. Let's see what we got." Wayne sat down next to him and perused the multiple tabs Kris had left open during his long, arduous excursion into job hunting.

"See?" Kris whined, "Where are all the entry-level openings?"

Wayne's left ear flicked as his eyes darted upward on the screen. "Oh, for the love of – this is freshman year all over again…" he groaned.

"What's that supposed to mean?" growled Kris, taking offense.

The wolf stood up again and sighed. "Dude! You haven't even narrowed your search down!"

"Narrowed… my search?" Kris was entirely oblivious to what the wolf meant. Without a word, Wayne retrieved his water bottle and then sat at the desk to type on the laptop.

The ostrich watched curiously as the wolf added a term to the search string, [-"5+ years"], then clicked the search button again. To Kris's astonishment, the screen's entries shrunk noticeably—several of the top results asked for little or no experience.

"Wait, wait, wait… what'd you do?!" Kris leaned over his friend's shoulder.

Wayne explained, "I added a filter. Now you'll see anything that did not explicitly ask for five or more years of experience," said Wayne as he stood up.

Kris immediately sat in his place. A bright joy spread across his feathered face as he scrolled through the new options. "Sweet! But… there's still a ton of things here that want some work experience and a lot that don't relate to any of my skills or interests."

"So, change the experience filter and add another to eliminate the jobs you don't care about. You don't really need me to tell you that, do you?" He saw the ostrich's expression and sighed before leaning over to tap at the keys again.

"Aw, this is awesome!" Kris practically crowed with enthusiasm. "Still over one hundred positions, and I'm a great match for any of 'em!"

Wayne moved back to his dresser and muttered. "Well, a great match if they don't need you to do anything with a spreadsheet..."

"I heard that," Kris snapped without turning from the laptop.

Wayne chuckled as he headed to the bathroom. "Whatever. I'm gonna take a shower."

"Alright, thanks, man," the ostrich called out as he adjusted his other searches as Wayne had done. As Kris updated his tabs, he heard the water run in the other room. The ostrich rubbed his winged hands together with glee. "Now...where do I start...?"

He quickly found a position that piqued his interest. Everything about the opening appealed to the ostrich, and he was confident that he had the necessary skills. However, the job was located in San Birdadino. He had lived his whole life in Pawston. Kris was intent on finding work but was not keen on moving across the country. That meant he had to adjust the search criteria more.

"Uhm... WAYNE?" the ostrich called over his shoulder.

<u>**Key Takeaways:**</u>

- Search engines work by finding keywords within the job posting. Choose your keywords wisely, it could be the difference between time savings and having to wade through a mound of unrelated jobs.
- Using keywords to screen out irrelevant job postings is a powerful time saver.
- Look up a guide for how to write Boolean search terms. Every job board is different, so make sure your guide applies to the site you are using.

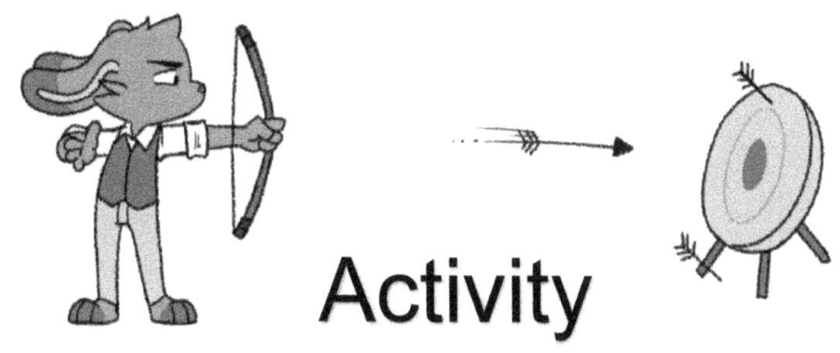

Activity

<u>**Writing Your Search Terms**</u>

Let's say you wanted to get a job as an office assistant somewhere in the state of New York. Let us see how many results pop out using the official NY job bank (aside: each state has an official job board. It is an overlooked resource for finding jobs).

Search: Office Assistant
Results: 49,439

Oh dear, that will not do. The search engine is looking through job postings for any mention of the words "office" and "assistant". The search results include job titles for things like Nurse Practitioner and Sales Executive Mobility [I have no idea what that means]. Let's make a simple change…

Search: "Office Assistant"
Results: 665

Much better. The quotation marks tell the search function to look for that specific phrase. But 665 is still too many to sort through manually, so let's add a filter. The NY state job bank includes office assistant jobs from anywhere in New York, including some from neighboring states. We can add a filter for just positions within New York and go a step further by selecting "Buffalo, NY" (let's pretend we live there).

Results: 58

There we go. Fifty-eight is a manageable number!
Keep in mind that every job search engine is different in what filters are built into its system. I have had the most success in reducing the search results by using job location, posting date, or a combination of both.

Give this a try! Type in an interesting job title into your job board of choice and see how many results are found. Look up a Boolean operator guide for that job board and begin experimenting with how to reduce the number of irrelevant results using search strings (what you type into the search bar) and search filters (additional search options on the job board, sometimes listed under "advanced search"). Write down any effective search strings so you may use them again at a later date.

CHAPTER TWO:
USE A PROFESSIONAL EMAIL ADDRESS

You should create a professional-sounding email address before applying for jobs. Why? Your email address could be the first thing a recruiter or hiring manager sees on your application. Vulgar, silly, or nonsensical email addresses might be judged harshly and impact the fate of your application.

"Well, Mr. Riparian," said the civet, grinning and reaching out a paw for the fish across from her to shake, "thank you for taking the time out of your busy schedule to come and interview today! That concludes our time together unless you have any questions for me."

The sturgeon took her paw and vigorously shook it up and down. His barbels quivered with nervous energy. "No questions," he chirped. "Thank you for having me!"

He'd been job searching for two months, and this interview had gone great! He had smiled. He had shaken her hand. He'd gotten the resume down, and the semi-formal business wear and he'd laughed and made her laugh – he was charismatic and professional, all despite being nervous.

A win like this was abnormal for Albus Riparian. His first interview had been at a tech start-up, and the interviewer – a grumpy turtle – seemed unimpressed when Albus had asked, "You want me to 'know Java?' Do you mean 'making coffee?'"

His second interview had been at a salon. Albus didn't understand how he flubbed his interview with the squirrely hairdresser. Was it because he'd forgotten to tuck in his shirt? Because he had no experience cutting hair? Or maybe it was because fish didn't have hair in the first place?

The sturgeon's third interview had been at a local grocery store. One of those high-turnover places, it constantly had a massive "NOW HIRING" sign stuck into the lawn out front. He assumed it'd be a shoo-in. Anyone with a pulse could land a job there. So, Albus attended an interview with a seagull manager while, admittedly, a little underdressed and a lot hungover. It wasn't a big deal, he thought. But it was. The awkward-looking, fifteen-year-old scruffy rat interviewed before him got a callback because he'd been bagging his groceries the next time Albus went shopping. But Albus' phone was dry.

It was hard to land a job as a fish out of water!

Mrs. Luwac, the civet, glanced over Albus's resume one last time. It was neat, professionally formatted, and all fit on one page. She really was impressed, for the most part. There was just one problem.

"Oh!" squeaked the civet. "Your resume is missing your email address."

"Oh!" echoed Albus, smiling wide and clasping his fins together at his lap. "Yes! I do not have one."

Mrs. Luwac arched an eyebrow. "You… don't have an email address?"

"Well, I have one, but…"

The civet blinked twice and offered a smile. "All of our candidates – and employees – need an email address on file."

"I have one," said the sturgeon. "But, you… need my email?"

Mrs. Luwac frowned. "Is that okay?"

A big glob of sweat quickly gathered at Albus's forehead. "Uh, yeah," he croaked. "That's okay!"

"Great! I can write it on here, for you, if you don't mind–" the civet grabbed a pen and uncapped it. The tip hovered right next to Albus's phone number. "What is it?"

Albus Riparian wiped his forehead with the back of his fin. The sturgeon only had one email address. He'd made it when he first moved onto dry land when he was sixteen. It was cool at the time. Really cool. But now…

The sturgeon pulled out his phone. Maybe he could make a new one? How long did that take? Thirty seconds? His frantic flippers scrolled through the apps secretly beneath Mrs. Luwac's desk.

"Mr. Riparian?" The civet was losing patience fast.

"Sorry…uh…I was trying to remember it."

"That's quite alright," said Mrs. Luwac. "Do you have it now for me?"

The sturgeon's face flushed with heat.

"Yeah," he said weakly, slumping at the torso. "Okay, it's…um…C-A-V,"

"C-A-V," echoed Mrs. Luwac.

"...I-A-R."

"...I-A-R, okay, got it."

"G-U-Z."

"Okay..." said Mrs. Luwac. "G-U-Z..."

The sturgeon sucked in a breath. "Z-L-E-R."

"Okay, Z-L-E-R."

"Six..."

"Oh. Six."

"...Nine."

"...Nine. Is that all?"

The sturgeon grit his teeth into a grin. "Yes! That is all!"

Mrs. Luwac stared at the email address she'd printed neatly beside Riparian's name: C-A-V-I-A-R-G-U-Z-Z-L-E-R-6-9.

She shot him a deadpan expression. "Your email address is "caviarguzzler69?"

Albus rubbed the back of his neck. It was hot in here. Why was it so hot in here? His sweaty face glistened in the fluorescent lighting. "Yes, uh. Yeah, that's it."

"Okay," said the civet.

"It's an inside joke," said Albus quickly. "It's...a fish thing."

"Mhm," said the civet. "What's the domain?"

"Domain?"

"The... You know. Gwhale, Owl-look..."

"Oh!" said Albus. "It's Hotsnail."

"Hotsnail."

"Yes. C-A-V-I-A-R-G-U-Z-Z-L-E-R-6-9 at Hotsnail dot com."

Mrs. Luwac scribbled the domain onto Albus's resume and abruptly stood.

"Thank you for your time," she said, opting for a polite nod over a second handshake. "We will... Definitely try to be in contact within two weeks."

"Okay, thanks!" said Albus, dipping his head before practically sprinting out the door.

He needed a new email... and a new job opportunity.

<u>**Key Takeaways:**</u>

* Applicant readers will assume things about who you are based on your email address.
* Consider the following when making a professional email address:
    o It is common to have your first name and last name, followed by some numbers.
    o Avoid using two-digit numbers. People may assume that the numbers stand for an important date in your life (e.g., birth year, graduation date). They may use that to guess your age or years of work experience.
    o Avoid using alternative spellings of your name. A recruiter may think the spelling is an error and then correct it to the usual spelling. You may never hear back from them.

* Honestly, just make a boring-sounding email address, and you are good to go!

Reflection

What's in an Email Address?

1. Go to your personal email account and gather email addresses of friends who are of similar age to you (not companies, older family members, etc.).

2. Create a new document. List the email addresses you gathered. Besides each email address, write a description of the person **based on their email address**. Consider the following:

   - Are they a professional-minded person?
   - Would they be effective in a job?
   - What stereotypical traits come to mind when reading their email address?
   - Is there anything unsettling or questionable about the email address?
   - How old are they (if there are any numbers present)?

3. Consider your own main email address…

    -    What does it say about you?
    -    What do you want others to think about when
         they read your email address?

4. Create a new email address if your answers to the
    above two questions are out of sync.

CHAPTER THREE:
DON'T USE A WORK COMPUTER

Never use a company computer or email address to apply for jobs. There is an increased chance of your employer discovering your job search if you are using company resources during working hours. You never know how your company will react to your job search.

Like most fresh graduates from Precinct 4 Sector 32, Norm was assigned to one of the mega-towers to sit at an ACI (Animal Computer Interface) all day and react to the computer's questions. Citizens from Precinct 4 were generally not considered intelligent enough to do any analytical work or athletic enough to do any work related to manual labor, both of which Norm would have loved to do.

Being young and not very forward-thinking, Norm signed a contract with the first company that approached them, not realizing that this would oblige them to stay with that company for at least 150 years, a timespan which exceeds the average lifespan of a capybara like them twice over. Not because it said so in the contract; no, this seemed to be an unwritten rule of Sector 32. If you leave your company before that time, you will likely have an "accident," falling down the floastreets, probably hitting a hover car on your way down, the repair your remaining family will have to pay for.

But Norm had a plan.

They would apply for a company in Precinct 5, Sector 30. The mega-corps and government in that area, while still authoritarian, were much more lenient. They could choose and apply for any job that they wanted. And Norm certainly had more confidence in their skills than the Ivory Tower Elites of Precinct 4 had. They would sneak through the Lowlands sewer systems out of Sector 32 and then take the four-day hike to Precinct 5. If they were lucky enough, maybe some of the Lowlanders would even help them with a ferry. Once they arrived in their new Precinct, they would get cheap accommodation, change their name, and start a new life. Nobody from Precinct 4 would ever find Norm there.

They looked at the clock at the far end of the depressing room. Grey cubicles were the only thing between their own and the clock. Not a single plant. No decorations. Only paper, ACIs, the occasional head of one of their larger coworkers, and the grey laminate panel walls of the cubicles.

Two more minutes until the break started

In their allocated five-minute breaks, the workers were allowed to use the ACIs for whichever leisurely activities they wanted. Instead of their usual quick gaming session, however, Norm would use the time to apply to four additional companies in Precinct 5 that they scouted over the last week. Norm already had one job offer but wanted to further their options with these companies. Then they'd wait another week or two for replies, prepare for the four-day hike, and leave the day they accepted the job offer.

Five days later, they had already gotten a reply. One of the four companies they were hopeful for returned an immediate job offer. Unconditional. The company was impressed by their application and test results and needed someone to start immediately. Norm did not need to think twice. They clicked the link in the mail, were forwarded to a company subpage, and hit accept. They were finally going to leave this damned place.

That's when the entire four-thousand-square-foot office space went black. All the neighboring mega-towers still had their lights on. Then, a blaring alarm went off, and red emergency lighting appeared.

"Undesirable employee action detected. Worker #3412-CAP, please make your way without any detours to floor 99 for disciplinary action."

Norm dropped down from their chair onto all fours.

That worker was Norm.

The speakers went off again.

"This is a reminder. Any activity during and outside of generously granted breaks on the Animal-Computer Interfaces and any other company-owned hardware is monitored at all times as stated by Sub-Clause 42212.2b of each worker contract."

Norm messed up. They should have used the ACI units in one of the cybercafes, even though they were a bit pricey. Now, their plan would be much more troublesome to carry out. Norm could hear their teeth chatter. A sign of fear and anxiety of capybaras. They had to escape.

They peeked outside of their cubicle. Nobody was moving. Norm would be spotted immediately, especially given their slightly chubby nature, but they had to move before someone would come "pick them up."

Norm opened the bottom and top buttons of their shirt, which was way too tight and made them feel even warmer now, given the situation. They started running on all fours towards the access door to the eastern stairwell. As they ran, they could hear company security arriving with the elevator and shouting directions towards Norm's cubicle. Norm was genuinely scared. All they ever heard about correctional action was that it was unforgettable, and nobody ever had to take a second such procedure.

They reached the access door and opened it slowly. They would certainly not get out through the main entrance. Thankfully, they knew there was a walkway to a neighboring building on the 56th floor. So, they just had to descend a couple of floors and could, hopefully, flee through that way.

"There they are! Stop them!" Norm heard from the office space as the access door slowly closed, and they hurried down.

The rain made the metal walkway extremely slippery. Equipment was placed on the neighboring tower's roof as some construction work was done outside of their companies' mega-tower.

Lucky for Norm. Unless they were not careful.

Norm could feel the wind blowing strongly at this height, cooling them off. Hover cars were whizzing past above as well as below. All colors from the omnipresent neon signs were refracting in the raindrops.

"Just a couple more steps. Then I'm as good as free." Norm tried to calm down.

"I'm not going to miss this rotten place."

Key Takeaways:

> - It is difficult to know how your employer will respond to your job search. This could range from lessening your work activities (e.g., reducing your hours, removing you from critical projects) to offering you more compensation to keep you. Err on the side of caution. You do not want your work situation to change because of some glances through job openings!
> - The company owns the information on its systems. If something goes wrong, they will have all the details of your job search and can use it against you. This is particularly true if the company believes you are using their resources to aid in your search (e.g., licensed software, intellectual property).

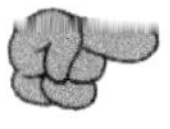 **Reallty Check.**

This story featured a dystopian society where mega-corporations actively monitor employees' online behaviors for employment contract violations. Modern non-governmental companies commonly have surveillance for issues regarding network security. As of the writing of this book it is uncommon for companies to use software or computer systems to detect if an employee wants to leave the company.

How an employer learns of an employee's job search is almost always either 1) the employee informs their employer about their job search; 2) the employee tells a co-worker who spreads the word throughout the workplace, which eventually makes it to a supervisor; or 3) a supervisor directly observes the employee searching for another job.

Reflection

Finding Alternatives

The most common reason for using a work computer for job searching is convenience.

Think of other ways to access a computer or materials you need for your job coarch. This might include using borrowed or public resources. Here are common places which could offer resources or support in your area:

- Public library
- School/University computer lab
- Community centers
- Friends or family

Always be mindful of how your information is stored. Do not leave sensitive information lying around in public spaces!

CHAPTER FOUR:
NETWORKING CAN PAY OFF

Networking is an acceptable way of finding a job. In fact, networking is a necessity in some industries. Jobs found through networking almost always speed up the process, whether getting your application to the top of the application stack, skipping a technical interview, or leading directly to a job offer. Sometimes, it all comes down to being in the right place at the right time.

Scooped Up by Packwolf Lupestripe

"No, I don't think we should run it," Ashley said, glowering at their editor. "It's all circumstantial. There's no proof."

"And let those people at The Star claim it?" their boss countered, his voice rising as he stood up from his chair. He focused on the young stoat, who shifted awkwardly in their seat.

"This is a major scoop, and you want them to just take it?" The crocodile banged his fist on the table, and Ashley jumped. "No! We're running it! End of story." He looked down at his desk and pressed a button on the intercom. "Sometimes I wonder why I promoted you," he snarled, his top lip revealing a row of jagged yellow teeth. "You're no journalist. You've got no bite, no instinct. You're just a pathetic little weasel."

Ashley grimaced in their chair, sinking into it so deeply that they almost became part of it. The intercom beeped.

"Yes sir?" the speaker crackled.

"Shelly, could you please escort Ashley out? I'm done with her."

"Right away, sir."

Ashley looked down at the floor, trying to avoid the crocodile's gaze. They had only been deputy editor at The Herald for six months but already felt out of their depth. This wasn't the first time he had gone over their head, but it didn't make it any less demoralizing.

They sighed before standing up, straightening their pencil trousers as they did. Ashley heard the office door open and, with an escape route secured, felt a sudden rush of courage.

"It's them," they said, staring squarely at the crocodile.

"Who's them?"

"Not her, them. 'I'm done with *them*,'" Ashley corrected him.

The crocodile scowled. "Him, her, them, it. I couldn't care less. Now get out!"

Ashley turned and strode away from the desk, tears forming in their eyes.

***

The characters blurred into incoherence as Ashley stared beyond the computer screen. Professional social media offered no solutions despite the countless hours spent on it.

They sighed. How they wished they could be a young reporter again, digging up stories and investigating leads instead of facing the crocodile's wrath every day. There had been a genuine camaraderie on the beat, even with rival journalists, as despite the competition, they were all purveyors of truth.

Ashley wondered whether any of their old contacts were still around. They dug out their phone and flicked through the address book as if trying to rekindle memories of a life once lived. Ashley recognized a few names, but what could they say? They had barely talked in the last five years. Would their numbers still be the same? Would they even remember them? And how would they react to a 'she' now being a 'they'?

Ashley sighed once again. It was worth a shot. Things had to change.

They steeled their resolve before formulating a message, hovering over the 'Send' button next to the name of the first contact. Nerves twisted in the pit of their stomach, but things became more manageable once they had sent the first one. Fifteen minutes later, seven messages had been sent. Only two had bounced back. They put their phone to one side and waited for a response.

Nothing was forthcoming until the following morning when they were awoken by the familiar chime of their cell phone. Ashley struggled to make out the message through blurry eyes before the letters honed into view.

"Hi Ashley, great to hear from you. Would you be free for coffee the day after tomorrow? There's much to discuss. Rhys xx"

Ashley's heart pounded as they typed a reply, wondering what to discuss. They suggested a time and a place to meet before sending the message. They had a lead.

***

The smell of roasted beans and cinnamon was overwhelming as Ashley entered the coffee shop. They grabbed a macchiato and scoured the room, hoping to find Rhys hiding beneath one of the woolen hats everyone was sporting.

It took Ashley a minute to locate the fox, who sat in a secluded booth at the back, hidden behind his laptop. He looked up and raised a paw in acknowledgment, the glint in his eye reminding Ashley of their early days as rookie journalists. They nodded and walked over.

"Great to see you again, Rhys," Ashley said.

"Likewise," the vulpine responded. "How are things?"

Ashley groaned before sitting down. "Not good, really," they said as they returned to those exhilarating early days. They had gotten into so many scrapes on The Herald's trainee scheme before he moved to The Star. Ashley still remembered the stinging feeling when he said he was leaving.

"Still at The Herald?"

"Aye, but I'm looking to get out. Hence the message. You?"

"At The Star, chief business editor, but I have news that may be interesting."

Ashley nodded nervously.

"The owners of The Herald aren't happy. They are losing money, and there have been allegations about mismanagement of the pension fund. I have been investigating for a while and believe your editor is involved. However, I don't yet have the proof I need."

Ashley stared, their mouth slowly dropping.

"I need more resources, someone who knows the company inside out. And when you sent me that text, I thought the timing was perfect."

Ashley blinked, not quite believing what they were hearing. The silence seemed to last forever.

"What do you think?" Rhys eventually asked.

"I...I...I don't know," Ashley said. "I can't just betray the paper."

"I'm not asking you to," Rhys continued. "But I am asking you to join me at The Star. My editor has already approved me, and we'd love to have you on board. You'd work with me on investigations as my equal, reporting directly to her."

Ashley stared at the fox, unsure what to do. They took another sip of coffee. The glint in his eye clinched it.

***

***HERALD CROC-KED BY PENSION FUND
SCANDAL - EDITOR CHARGED WITH FRAUD***

Ashley looked down at the mocked-up front page
and smiled. It had taken six weeks, but they had
followed the trail and pieced the story together. Their
eyes wandered to the byline, which credited Ashley
and Rhys—their first significant scoop at The Star,
hopefully the first of many.

"What do you think?" their editor asked behind her
desk.

Ashley turned to Rhys and caught his trademark
glint. Their smile became a grin. "I think we should run
it."

<u>**Key Takeaways:**</u>

- It is possible to get a job based entirely on networking connections. It is most common to happen in smaller companies and for senior-level positions.
- It takes time to network. You either must establish a personal network or become involved in a group (e.g., alumni club, community organization, online community).
- You must find the right balance between networking and submitting traditional job applications. Networking has a chance of landing you a job, but the time and effort needed for networking could mean that you miss great opportunities you could have applied for.

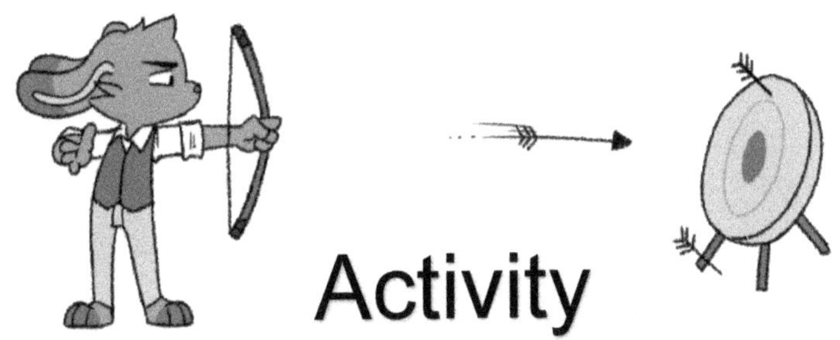

Building a Network

1. Take out a sheet of paper or open a new document on your computer. Write down people you know who are of working age. These people could be family, friends, old co-workers, classmates, members of your community, and anyone else interested in your success and well-being.

2. Map out their past and current work. Take note of people who have a connection to your industry of interest.

3. Start talking to people on your list. Let them know you are looking for a job in "X" and ask if they have any advice on how to get into the industry.

4. Begin with people who are or were most connected to your industry of interest. After this initial group, reach out more broadly.

5. Keep in mind your relationship with the other person and their ability to create opportunities for you. For example, did you go to school with someone who works for an exciting company with an employee referral program who is willing to put in a good word for you? Go for it! How about your distant cousin that "has a friend" who works at that same company? Maybe not much will come out of that connection…

Other Notes:
- Some professions have notable membership organizations. Look them up! Sometimes they are worth joining so you can connect with other members. Also, these organizations may have public job boards.

- Some industries have formal networking events (most common with entertainment). These will differ in usefulness depending on the industry and who is gathered. The way to make the most out of formal networking events is to come ready to connect (e.g., having relevant talking points and contact information ready to hand out) and to establish rapport quickly within the conversation. It is better if the other person develops an interest in your success, opposed to seeing you as a meat bag capable of performing work.

CHAPTER FIVE:
DON'T LIE

Tell the truth when describing yourself on your resume and during interviews. There is a fine line between stretching your qualifications and lying about them. You will be found out quickly during a technical interview when you cannot do the things you claimed you could. Also, people who hire are sensitive to lying. They will reject your application if they think it is bogus.

Phasmo-no-bia by Brian Renadette

Nora never thought "exorcism" would be on the to-do list when it came to flipping houses.

As their van pulled into the driveway of 44 Hemlock Lane, Nora glanced over at their two passengers. Seated next to them was a stern-looking lion, his muzzle graying from his many years working in the local church. Without a word, he reached to his neck, pulled out the rosary tucked underneath the collar of his priest's robes, and breathed deeply. Behind the two was a sheep, easily half the lion's age but clad in the same priestly robes, clinging anxiously to the back of the seats. Because there weren't any back seats, he had the pleasure of sitting with the assorted house-flipping tools Nora owned.

"Well, this is it," Nora smirked. "Who knew driving out the spirits of the restless dead required an old priest, a young priest, and a house flipper?"

The lion nodded in agreement and turned back to look at the lamb. "Thomas, grab the things and meet us in front of the house."

"Yes, Father Mercer," Thomas said as he rummaged through the mess of tools in the back.

The three of them were gathered outside the house's front door a minute later. Despite the house's age, the outside was clean and well-maintained, all thanks to Nora's preliminary cleaning: trimmed shrubs, a freshly seeded lawn, and a swept porch. However, a quick look through any of the windows would show plenty more to be done.

"Alright," Nora said. "So, this is going to be a basic exorcism, Father?"

"Judging by what you told us, yes," Father Mercer replied. "Your description of what happened last night makes it sound like a basic poltergeist. However, I've been getting up in years, so Thomas will be handling most of the exorcism. He joined as a pastor a few months ago, and he told me he's done several exorcisms in the past."

"Yeah, nothing too serious, I'm sure," Thomas added.

"Well, I'll trust your judgment, you two. Flashlights on, we're going in."

As Nora opened the front door, the group's flashlights dimly illuminated a living room in transition. While most of the room had been untouched for months, there were signs of attempts to clean it up. Heavy layers of dust that only coated a few square feet of flooring and filled trash bags that were only a few days old littered the floor. But perhaps most notable was the message on the wall directly across from the door, written in a deep crimson.

LEAVE MY HOME

"Yeah, I think that writing alone is enough evidence of a haunting," Nora remarked. "If only that ghost were a bit kinder, then I could try to convert this place into a self-supporting blood bank!"

Father Mercer chuckled. "That would certainly be an interesting project. Now, the spirit should have noticed us enter their residence, so we should be ready. Thomas, are you ready to cleanse this house?"

Before Thomas could respond, the group's flashlights started to flicker violently.

"I hope you're going to say 'Yes,'" Nora said, "because here it comes!"

The furniture in the room began to shake as house-flipping supplies started to rise into the air. Suddenly, a half-used can of paint flung itself at the trio, causing them to scatter. Thomas ducked behind an old sofa, fumbled in his pocket, and pulled out a crucifix.

"The power of Christ compels you! The power of Christ compels you!!" he began shouting.

"Now isn't the time to reenact some movie! Drive the spirit out!" Mercer shouted back from the bookcase he was using for cover. In the corner of the room, Nora had grabbed an old standing lamp and was using it to bat away tiles they had earlier brought to wall the bathroom.

"I... uh..." Thomas stammered. "I didn't think there'd be a ghost here!"

"What do you mean, Thomas? All the signs were there," Mercer shouted back, ducking as a vase shattered over his head.

"I didn't think they really existed! I don't actually know how to stop hauntings!"

"Of all the times to learn one of my priests can't deal with a blasted ghost! What next, do you not know the classic verses!?"

"Well…"

As Mercer continued to berate the junior priest, the shaking in the room began to subside as the remaining floating objects fell to the floor. The tongue-lashing only ended when Nora chimed in.

"Father, on the wall!"

Mercer and Thomas looked at the wall where Nora was pointing to find a new message painted in dark blood that looked freshly spilled.

YOUR CHURCH NEEDS AN EXORCIST?

The three stood silent as they took in the message.

"I… I suppose so, spirit," Mercer called out, hoping the spirit was listening.

A light breeze filled the room as a phantasmal figure appeared before them. Aside from being see-through, the spectral mouse looked pretty normal, with his fur being matted in points from old age.

"If you need a priest," the mouse said. "I'd be happy to apply for the position. It beats being stuck in this old home, doing nothing but driving out squatters and real estate agents."

"Wait," Father Mercer said. "Nora, do you know who owned this house before you bought it?"

Umm…" Nora thought. "I think the papers said it was someone by the last name of Carlson. Joseph Carlson, that was it."

"Father Carlson! I remember hearing about him several years ago," said Mercer. "He had retired from the church over in Doveington after serving as its head for about forty years. I didn't know he spent his last years here." Mercer turned to Carlson. "Father, I would happily have your assistance working for us.

Carlson smiled. "It would be my honor. May I ask what we'll be doing with the one I'm replacing?" Carlson motioned to Thomas, who was still ducked behind the side of the sofa.

"Oh, there's plenty of cleaning back at the church that he can do until he actually learns the basics of being a priest."

"Well, this has been quite a night," Nora said. "But Father Carlson, I do have one question."

"What is it, child?" he asked.

"Do you think it's worth tearing down the wall between the two bedrooms to make one large one?"

<u>**Key Takeaways:**</u>

- If a reviewer thinks you are lying about something, they will throw out your application.
- You cannot fake your way through a skills assessment.
- Some states and/or jobs have a 90-day probation period where they can revoke your contract without much effort. Even if you lie your way in, you could be let go rather quickly.

Reflection

How Bad is Lying?

It is common to inflate your credentials in a resume or during an interview, but you must be careful about how far you go. For example, you could tell an interviewer something outlandish that causes them to test your knowledge at a more advanced level than they normally would have.

Take out a sheet of paper or open a new document on your computer.

- Think about a time when you caught someone telling a lie. How did your opinion of that person change? Write down an explanation of the situation and how it made you think or feel at the time.

- Think about a time when you felt suspicious about another person. Write a description of the situation and consider the following questions:

    - Did you treat that person differently than you normally do? If yes, how?
    - How did you feel about that person at that moment?
    - Did you do anything to confirm your suspicions?
    - Did your suspicion change your opinion of that person after the situation (i.e., long-term effects)?

Consider your above responses. How might a recruiter or interviewer think or feel about you if they thought you were lying?

CHAPTER SIX:
BE MINDFUL WHEN USING SOCIAL MEDIA

Every profession has a presence on social media. Become active within that community by posting relevant content, interacting with other professionals, or just staying current on happenings within the field. It is not unheard of for companies to look up applicants on social media before a significant interview. Keep your social media professional; you will be judged harshly if your content is inappropriate, controversial, or unsafe for work.

Boxed In by Packwolf Lupestripe

"…And that is why I believe I would be the perfect fit for your company," Lewth said, folding his wings around his body confidently.

The managing director nodded before glancing down at the resume on his desk. "Do you have any experience of the dark?" he inquired. "I don't see much here other than you like to go spelunking on weekends."

Lewth's confidence waivered as the field mouse looked up with a stern expression written across his face. "I… I… I grew up in a cave," he stammered. "I'm a bat, after all. And I am sure your warehouse isn't as complicated as some caves I have explored."

"Uh-huh," the field mouse said, unconvinced. "I'm going to need more than that. We employ a lot of bats here. Our wine is susceptible to both light and temperature, so it must be stored quickly and efficiently. How do I know you aren't going to drop a bottle? They cost over two hundred bucks each."

Lewth gulped as he racked his brain for an answer, but before he could speak, the field mouse continued.

"Perhaps you could use one of those boxes you designed, the one you advertised on social media. I did find it fascinating. Tell me, what is an 'afterdark' account?" He smiled.

Lewth felt like someone had punched him before a blush spread to his cheeks.

"Wh-What do you mean? How do you know about that?"

The field mouse maintained his composure as he watched the bat squirm in his seat. "Are those boxes designed to put folks in? To restrain them? Is that part of some game?"

Lewth flushed visibly as the field mouse hid a smile behind his paw. He looked down at the floor, wishing it would swallow him whole. He knew the mouse knew the answers to those questions and all the images he must have seen. He groaned, desperately wanting to be dismissed from the interview, but the field mouse obviously wasn't done with him yet.

"Well?" his interviewer asked impatiently.

"I... I... I don't know," the bat replied feebly. "A friend asked me to make it. I wanted to help." The bat looked up at the mouse, who was well aware of his discomfort. The silence seemed to last forever as Lewth felt his heart pounding like a death knell. Eventually, he just had to say something for the awkwardness to end. "How did you find out?"

The field mouse replied, "Let's just say, when you're interacting with the company, it might be best to check from which account you're posting."

Lewth's eyes went wide as he realized his mistake.

The field mouse continued, "I was impressed with your contributions to our online community. Some of your ideas were very innovative. You clearly know the industry, and your professional account was very convincing. It's just a shame you revealed more than you intended to..."

Lewth nodded meekly. He had wanted this job so badly, and now, one moment of carelessness had ruined his chances. He watched helplessly as the interviewer's attention seemed to shift.

"I'm not sure some of the staff will look at you in the same light again, but that may be an issue for later. So, tell me about the boxes."

Lewth sighed, knowing he couldn't worm himself out of the discussion. "What would you like to know?"

"Could you design something for the bats, something they could use to carry the bottles to the shelves? It would protect the wine and boost efficiency."

Lewth couldn't believe what he heard but decided to follow it anyway. "I could certainly try," he admitted. "They would be much smaller, and we'd need to test them, but it's possible. It would only take a few days, maybe a week."

The field mouse nodded, an idea forming in his mind. "Okay, Lewth. How about this? We'll employ you as a consultant for the first three months and see how things go. If it works out, then we'll look to hire you permanently. Does that work for you?"

Lewth blinked, incredulous at being offered the job, albeit in a roundabout way. "So, none of my private life matters?"

"You hardly kept it private," the field mouse chuckled, "but no. Many employers would disagree, but what you do in your own time is your business. Just be more discreet in the future. And please delete the offending response."

"Yes sir," Lewth said, relief coursing through his body.

"See you on Monday," the field mouse continued as he filed the resume in one of his desk drawers.

"Thank you," Lewth said as he stood up and gently shook hands. He started towards the door.

"Lewth," he heard behind him. The bat turned around.

"When I asked whether you had experience with the dark, why didn't you mention the blindfolds? It would have been far more convincing."

Lewth blushed again.

<u>**Key Takeaways:**</u>

> • Consider creating separate social media accounts, one for work and the other for personal use. Keep a clear separation between the two.
> • If you are active in not safe for work content [this is a judgment-free zone], consider going under an alias while interacting in that space. Do not include identifiable information or personal pictures while using the alternative account. You would not want a potential employer to "bump" into your alternative profiles!
> • It is best to interact with companies through email instead of social media. Most company social media accounts are managed by marketing staff. Marketing cannot help you with hiring questions.

 **Reality Check:**

This story featured an interviewer who knew of the private activities of the candidate being interviewed. I want to make this clear: candidates have a right to be interviewed free of sexual harassment, regardless of the known (or assumed) gender, sexual orientation, relationship status, sexual activities, etc. of the candidate. Seek legal counsel if you experience sexual harassment during any step of the hiring process.

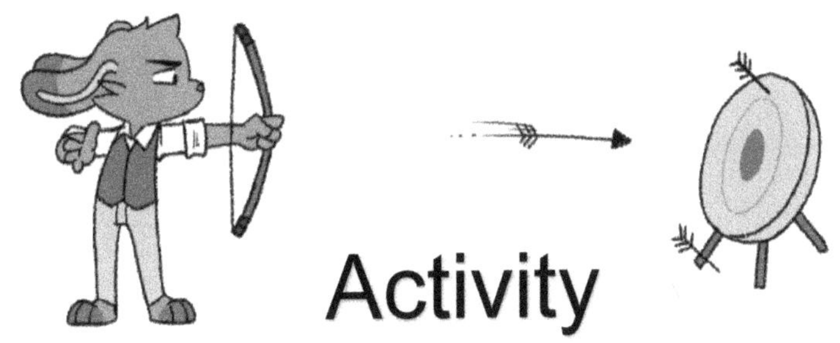

<u>Setting Up Your Social Media</u>

1. Look at where jobs are posted. If they are posted on social media, note which platforms and who is posting them (e.g., is it a company account or a specific person within the company).

2. Look at where notable people in the Industry post. Which social media platforms are they posting on and how have they built their social media profile (e.g., cover pictures, profile picture, description, length of message)?

3. Create an account on the most used social media platform. Build your profile so it matches the visuals of what other people do within your target industry.

4. Start participating in the industry's social media space. Stay current on industry trends by reading posts, responding to other's posts with questions, reposting information you think is notable, and

creating content relevant to the community.

5. CRITICAL: Always check which account you are posting from when on social media. Do not mix your personal account with your professional account.

CHAPTER SEVEN:
THE FIVE STAGES OF HIRING

Hiring systems commonly have five stages: resume review, recruiter screening call, technical interview or skill assessment, interview with the team to figure out if you are a good fit with their culture, and job offer. Do not get emotionally attached to a job prospect until you enter the technical interview stage.

Aiming High by William Dingo

Melati could tell something wasn't quite right when she entered the apartment. Aromatic spices usually permeated the kitchen when she came home, accompanied by sounds of bubbling pots or traditional singing on the radio. It was quiet, and there was no hint of dinner to come.

"Mom?" The kookaburra called out, head flicking about to detect any sounds apart from the muted traffic three stories down.

"Mel, I'm in the bedroom," her mother called out. "Dad's not home yet."

Her tone wavered and threatened to break. Melati was immediately worried. Her mother was a powerhouse and an impenetrable fortress. What could have happened?

She scuttled to her mother's room, and the young bird chirped uncertainly when she saw her mother, Indah, perched on the bed, hugging her knees, talons crossing over the side. She looked at Melati with red eyes. Tissues lay scrunched up and scattered around one side of the bed, while paperwork lay on the other side underneath her laptop.

Melati dropped her backpack onto the floor and hurried to sit beside her. "Mother? What happened?"

"Just…" Indah sighed, reaching for another tissue to dab her eyes. "I got a 'thank you for applying' response. I didn't quite get the top pick."

"That big job you were going for?" Melati dutifully grabbed clean tissues and corralled the used ones into a bin. Then she hopped up onto the bed to comfort her with a hug. They held each other as they sat, appreciating the quiet moment and reassurance. Melati waited for that 'daughter sense' to know when her mom felt comfortable talking. It took a little while before Melati felt comfortable enough to pry. "What's it like going through the process?"

Indah huffed, her warm breath blowing over Melati's feathers. "It's a lot of heartache and trouble, so be prepared. I'm used to this, but I got emotional when I saw the email."

Melati nodded despite being unsatisfied with the answer. "But really, what happens?"

"I don't know about other fields, but it can be tough at my level. Acute care assessment and crisis intake teams aren't just graduates, you know?" There was a brief pause where Indah's reluctance seemed to erode. "Are you sure you want to know? It's not that interesting."

Melati nestled her beak into her mother's side. "It's too late. I'm already comfortable."

Indah laughed and gently preened the feathers on Melati's head. Her usual 'I love you' habit hadn't changed since she was a chick. Her tone switched to that of a chirpy tutor. "Alright. The first step to applying for this job is to make a resume and cover letter."

"How long was yours?"

"My job is a very extreme example. I had to submit a CV, that's short for curriculum vitae, a long-form description of all my work achievements. CV's are common in my line of work, but for everything else, you only need a one or two-page resume. Maybe a half-page cover letter if they ask for it."

Melati looked at the papers on the bed, and her eyes boggled.

Indah giggled in amusement, threatening to bellow into a full cackle. "No, ignore those. I was just caught in the middle of research. All the applications that pass the criteria are reviewed and screened. It would probably get tossed if you had this many pages for a resume."

Melati relaxed a little. "Then someone calls you up for an interview?"

"More or less. Sometimes, you get a recruiter to screen you first. When I first applied at a private clinic, they used a recruiter to weed candidates out after the resume screen. I thank the gods divine that I don't have to face them anymore. The recruiters only knew general information about the job. They asked for what qualifications or training I had completed, and it felt sterile. There was no interest or inquiry to anything I asked, and I felt like I was a parrot for my resume.”

Melati scoffed but wondered how she would fare against a recruiter. “Shouldn’a done that,” she mumbled, trying to be supportive.

“After you survive the recruiter, you get the real interviews, maybe one or two. I go through two or more interviews for every job application nowadays.”

Melati’s feathers puffed out in concern. “That’s a lot of interviews for just one job.”

“It’s a specialist position. The board wanted to be sure I knew what I was talking about.”

“You’ll do a good job. You always do,” Melati reassured her mother. “You’ve raised three kids as a single mother and still managed to get us through college before you remarried.”

“Except you,” she tutted.

“Mom! That’s the worst way to say I haven’t yet graduated!” Her feathers puffed out again as she stared accusingly.

Her mother just laughed. “When you get to the interview, they have all those lovely questions about who you are, why you’re applying for the position, your strengths, and “tell me about a time when…” questions. You could listen to podcasts and watch videos all day long telling you how to deal with those questions, but nothing beats experience.”

Indah leaned on the headboard resignedly. "And then your final interview might be the team interview. Your last chance to impress everyone."

Melati imagined a room filled with her college friends competing for the same job. It felt too much like reality TV. "What's the team interview? Do you interview with all the other candidates?"

Indah looked confused for a moment before chuckling. "No, no. I should have said, 'Interview with the team.' The department heads and a registrar interviewed me. They asked me how I would work with a complex presentation or improvements I had in mind for the position. Another question they asked was how I delegated work under pressure or time constraints. At that stage, they usually want to know what to expect and how well they'll work with you. The focus on the interview significantly moves from technical skills to how you fit with the team and how you fit in with the workplace culture."

Melati nodded and leaned in to embrace her mother again. "So… what happens after that?" she prompted.

"It's pretty simple. They send you an offer letter, and you either accept it, reject it, or you try to negotiate for better terms in the offer."

"You already earn good money. Why do you want this job so badly?"

Indah smiled. "This is a similar job, but with better benefits. They need someone who has experience in crisis care, a lot of experience. And I have it."

"How many of these job applications have you gone through?"

Indah shrugged a wing. "I think this is the seventh time I've gone through it over three years."

Melati pulled back. "That can't be true! Why?"

Indah didn't answer for a moment as she opened her laptop and clicked through a few web pages, then twisted the screen around so Melati could see the salary.

The younger kookaburra's eyes widened, and her beak hung open. "Holy goose poop!"

Key Takeaways:

- The five stages are: resume review, recruiter interview, assessment/technical interview, workplace fit interview, and job offer.
- These are the traditional steps. Some industries and/or jobs might combine stages, others may add additional rounds to a stage. For example, technical jobs may include several rounds of technical interviews to ensure that candidates have the necessary skills. By comparison, food service jobs may host a walk-in interview day that combines several steps into one or remove a stage entirely.
- Read through the job posting or ask the recruiter for more details on the hiring process.
- The goal of each stage is to reduce the number of applicants based on how well the applicant meets the job requirements.
- The further you go, the more likely it is that you will get a rejection notice.
- It is common to hear nothing back from the company if your resume was rejected during the first stage. Do not wait to hear back from them to start looking at other jobs. Just take your wonderful self and go apply elsewhere!

Reflection

Recording What You Have Learned

1. Take out a fresh sheet of paper or open a blank document on your computer. Separate the page into five columns and label each column as follows: Apply, 1st Call, Skill Call, Fit Call, and Offer.

2. Go about your job search.

3. Whenever you finish a step in the hiring process with a company, do these three things: Stop, Reflect, and Write.
    *   Stop: Take a break from what you are doing, pull out this sheet of paper, and look at what you have written in the relevant column.
    *   Reflect: Ask yourself this: What have I learned going through this hiring step for this job prospect? If you are in a negative space when answering this question, then take care of yourself first and then come back to the

question. Go on a walk, eat something, take a shower, whatever you do to reset. Reflect on your experience only when you are ready!

- Write: Summarize your answer to the reflection question. You can change what you already have written in your columns or add something new. Keep it constructive.

4. CRITICAL: Do this for every step, even after accepting the offer letter. You will apply for more than one job in your lifetime, believe it or not. You will go through the offer process again, so you might as well have notes from the past to help with future opportunities.

The purpose is to build a note sheet that lists the lessons you have learned. These can be powerful reminders if your job search drags on [which I hope does not happen to you!].

CHAPTER EIGHT: STANDARD PAGE SIZE, B&W RESUME, PLEASE!

Ensure your resume is a standard page size (8.5 x 11 inches), fills a single page (double-sided okay), and is in black and white. It is customary to print out resumes for review before an interview, so you will be at a disadvantage if your printed resume is hard to read.

Resume the Resumé Search by Rixor Amsel

Mr. Howard was serious.

He didn't think it was a bad thing, to be serious. A red deer stag, he wore a well-groomed mane, and his clothes – always a vest, dress shirt, and tie – were well-ironed. Appearances were everything: during annual antler shedding, he took his holiday, and when his antlers were fully grown, he ensured that they were always correctly polished and pointed.

It wasn't vanity. It was respect, both for himself and for others. Why present oneself to the world in any other way than one's absolute best?

As the hiring manager for Caribou Connections Cooperative, Mr. Howard had earned somewhat of a reputation: people seemed to think he was just a bit of a tyrant. Of course, he'd disagree with that assessment: he cared deeply for his company and coworkers and wanted only the best joining their team – he wasn't trying to be off-putting! He was trying to be professional! It didn't change that, given his reputation, few people applied.

The company's HR representative had suggested Mr. Howard hold walk-in interviews for the newest entry-level opening. Mr. Howard agreed. After setting up advertisements, clearing his schedule, and sending out emails, Mr. Howard had set a date, March 15th, for drop-in interviews.

Today was that day.

It was 11:13 AM – two hours since drop-ins started – and nobody had come yet. The stag occupied himself by fidgeting with paperclips and browsing profiles on Lynx-Inn.

That was until there was a knock at the door of his office. The red deer cleared his throat. "Please, come in!"

A bee walked in – tall, yellow-black, professionally clothed in a stark-white blouse, long black skirt, and matching black blazer. One of her four hands carried a briefcase. A different one stretched out to shake Mr. Howard's hoof. "It's so good to meet you," she said with a grin.

"Likewise," said Mr. Howard. "Thank you for coming! And your name is?"

"Wanda," said the bee. "I really appreciate you taking the time to do this!"

"It's my pleasure. Well, Wanda, please do have a seat!"

The bee carefully pulled out the chair across from Mr. Howard and plopped down on her abdomen.

This was impressive. An excellent first impression was a good sign. The bee seemed polite, competent, and well put-together.

"Wanda," said Mr. Howard, "to start, do you happen to have a resume I can look at?"

"Of course." Without delay, she heaved her big, leather briefcase onto the desk. The stag watched as she undid the clasps and pulled out a stack of five-inch thick paper.

"What is this?" asked Mr. Howard.

"My resume," she said.

"Your resume," repeated Mr. Howard, eyes wide as he leafed through the mound of paper.

"That is correct," said the bee sweetly.

"Er," said Mr. Howard. He glanced over the cover page. "It says here that you've managed…thirty-five *thousand* employees?"

The bee nodded. "Yup! That's right!"

"And…"

"So," Wanda happily buzzed, "pages one through twenty are about me. My mission statement, my highlights, my hobbies, my interests, that sorta thing."

Mr. Howard swallowed down a lump that had formed in his throat.

"…Twenty-one through seventy-four detail my education! K-12, college, and all my clubs, awards, and extracurriculars… And seventy-five through three-hundred-and-two are all about my work experience. I have a *lot* of work experience."

"…Well," said Mr. Howard, adjusting his tie and pushing up his glasses. "I'm… going to need some time to look through all of this. Can I call you back here some other time?"

"Certainly!" Wanda grinned. "I look forward to hearing from you."

"...Yes." The stag watched the bee grab her suitcase and exit his office.

***

An elephant came in after Wanda. He was well-dressed, quiet, and experienced, but above all, he was tall. Despite being one sheet, the resume he handed Mr. Howard was 42.5 by 55 inches large – five times bigger than a standard piece of paper! The stag had to lay the massive work on the floor to read any of it!

***

After a long day of similar interviews and similarly inadequate resumes, a bullfrog walked inside.

"Thank you for holding these," she said, well-dressed and polite. "It's a pleasure to meet you."

"Can I see your resume?" asked an exasperated Mr. Howard.

"Sure thing," croaked the frog. She pulled out a resume and handed it to the stag. His tired eyes read it over.

One page. Black and white. Printed on standard paper without any mistakes or errors. "This is your resume?"

The frog's throat wobbled as she smiled. "Yes, it is; I know it's a little short, but–"

"When can you start?"

<u>**Key Takeaways:**</u>

- Although recruiters almost always view resumes on their computer, it is still common for interviewers to print your resume to read through and write notes.
- Many interviewers print resumes just before an interview. Your resume needs to look good when printed because it acts as a first impression for the interviewer.
- Some offices have low quality printers, so make sure your resume uses standard resolution and black and white images (e.g., text, symbols).
- It is important to use a format that will not change when opened by another program. PDF is the safest file type because Word may modify your layout when printing. This could turn your resume from a visual work of art to garbage in an instant.

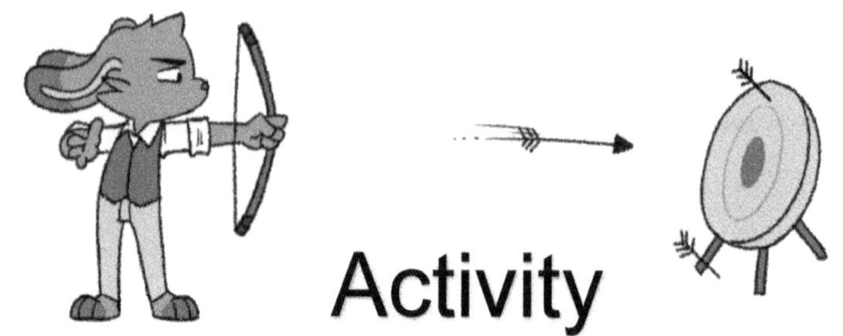

Activity

Resume Print Test

Do a print test when you are done crafting your resume. Change your printer settings to the lowest quality: Lowest resolution, black and white (no gray scaling), etc. Look at the low-quality printout and adjust your resume as necessary. The goal is to have your resume be as presentable as possible.

CHAPTER NINE:
INCLUDE A RESUME SUMMARY

You should place important information at the top of your resume. The goal is to help recruiters find relevant knowledge, skills, or abilities quickly. Remember, recruiters may be reviewing hundreds of applications for the job. Details buried in text could be missed, and your application could get put aside.

Resume Potential by Louis Williams

Roger paced in front of Katrine as she read over his resume. The small kitchen in his apartment was just big enough for him to take three steps and turn. His thick retriever tail would brush against the cabinet every time he turned around, making a barely audible swish. Katrine's black triangular ears were pinned against her skull. Her red marker was out, and it slashed away at his resume.

Each red mark he felt was a slash in his soul. He stared at the kitchen floor, trying his best not to hear the pen scraping along the carefully selected paper, marking out each line as wrong. Insufficient. The sounds of his feet marking pace, his gentle tail swishing against the cabinet door, played a backbeat against his breath, the anxiety he felt in his chest as Katrine continued making marks on his resume.

"I graduate in three months," he said, still pacing.

"Uh huh," Katrine replied.

He turned, his tail swished against the cabinet, and then spoke, "I've been applying for jobs for the past two. I haven't gotten a lot of callbacks."

"Uh huh," Katrine said again, her red pen marking another part on the resume. Her feline muzzle twisted into a sneer of concentration. Her tail twitched behind her as she stared at the paper before her.

"If you can just-" he began.

"I'm working on it," she replied. "Almost done. Don't chew yer fur off over it." She looked up and smiled at him, as big and professional as she could muster. "It's not wise to rush the HR manager."

Roger sighed and stood still, staring at the floor. He couldn't bring himself to look her in the eye. Not yet. When Katrine lowered the paper, she smiled. "There now. I think we can work with this." She said, twisting the resume over back to him.

The paper was in his paws in a flash. "What?" He asked, looking down on it. "I'm confused." The resume looked nothing like what he had handed her. She had marked out his job experience section and drawn an extensive line pointing downward to indicate it was being shoved to the bottom of the page. The Awards and Certifications section, originally under the job experience portion, was pointed upwards. Even his bio had been marked through.

"About what?" she asked, her tail had stopped twitching. A smile was in her ears now, one that reflected on her face.

"I mean, you're saying my work experience should be further down? Why?"

"Do you know how many resumes they're getting for this position?"

"I don't know, forty or fifty, I guess."

"Forty or fifty from one job board alone. Valcope put this entry-level Database Developer position on three different boards. Not to mention on their own website. They're going to have a mountain of applicants. Probably hundreds."

He swallowed hard, a knot forming in his throat. "Then how do I even get noticed?"

"Well," she smiled, "they're going to take a moment to skim over it and move on, right? Your resume should make them stop looking and want to ask you questions. You will want to intrigue them. The more intrigued they are, the better your chances are for an interview."

"So, that's why you're saying my awards and certifications should be higher?"

She nodded. "Your only work experience really, besides the one internship, is a fast-food place and a janitor. That isn't very strong. So, these awards look much better: Making the Dean's list, winning this…what is this Db Sweepstakes?"

Roger beamed with pride for a moment. "One of my professors held a contest at school for Computer Scientists. Create the most complex and workable database. We were each given a different business. Mine was a burger joint. I made mine using PL/SQL to help interface on the backend with the ordering application on the fake website and PGQL for the graphs and reports. Essentially, all the professor had to do was click one button, and everything generated."

"You see," she said, tapping the paper for emphasis. "That one part. The Db Sweepstakes. That made me want to ask you a question. If this were my company, I'd probably call you in for an interview just for that."

"So, what about my bio didn't you like?"

"Well, it looks like you just looked up industry buzzwords and threw them in. You want there to be industry lingo, yes. But you don't want just empty buzzwords. You also want it to look professional. And this other one, where you say your intention is to, and I quote, 'conquer the world with databases'? Why do you even have that?"

"I figured I'd get their attention with humor." His ear tipped a smile at her as he spoke.

Katrine's feline ears twitched. She barely held them up, but her tail tip twitched harder. "It kind of looks like you're not serious about getting a job," she sighed. "I wouldn't use that. Ever."

"So," Roger said, his tail wagging as he held up the resume, "I make these changes, and then I'll get some callbacks, huh?"

"Perhaps," Katrine replied. "Now, let's see your cover letter."

Roger tilted his golden-furred head in that comical universal canine expression of confusion. "Cover letter?"

<u>**Key Takeaways:**</u>

- Recruiters may not know much about the job they are hiring for and rely heavily on language from the job posting. Think about what is emphasized in the job posting when building your resume.
- Create a summary section at the top of your resume, below your name/address but above your work experience. Write two or three sentences that cover what you think the recruiter is looking for.
- Including a summary section makes your resume easier to adjust for each job application. Now you just need to rework two or three sentences with keywords as opposed to updating your entire work history.
- A summary section contributes towards the reader's first impression of you. It could be the difference between being put aside or moving forward in the process.

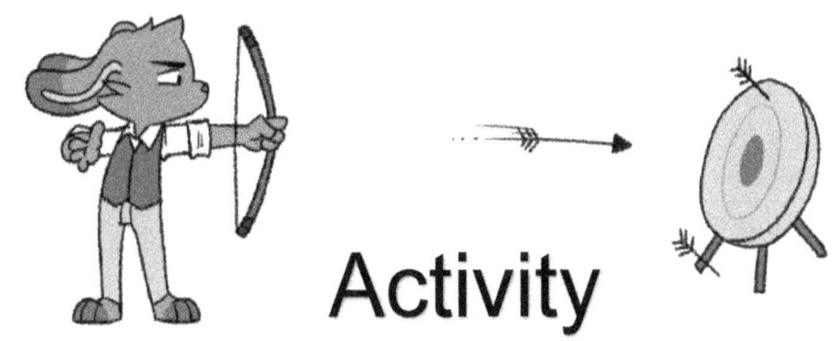

Identifying Key Words in Job Postings

1. Find five jobs that use the job title you are looking to apply for. Save those job postings as a PDF. These jobs do not have to be viable leads; they could be for jobs that are too far away from where you live or have already been filled. You are just looking for the language used to describe the jobs.

2. Open a blank document on your computer. Create four columns and label them Knowledge, Skill, Ability, and Other.

   - Knowledge = Things you know or could learn from reading a book.
   - Skill = Things that you can do or take practice to get good at.
   - Ability = Things that are part of who you are (like your personality) or something you are born with.

- Other = Whatever is not covered by the previous three. This could be lifting a 50 lb box, being able to see certain colors, or having a license to drive a commercial vehicle.

3. Look through one of the job postings you saved and place all the listed details into one of the four columns. Do this for each of the job postings you saved, each as its own document.

4. Compare what you wrote between the job postings. What details overlap across the jobs? Create one more four-column document and place the overlapping details in the appropriate column.

5. Open your resume and add space near the top of the page for your summary section. This could be just under your name or where makes sense given your layout. There should be enough space for three sentences.

6. Write a summary of yourself that includes the overlapping details of the jobs you reviewed. Do not lie [Chapter 5]; be honest with what you include in the summary.

Think of this as your base summary. Feel free to adjust the summary to speak to unique details that are listed in the specific job you are applying to.

CHAPTER TEN:
MAKE A ROBOT RESUME

Make two resumes: one for living reviewers and another for uploading into computer systems (a.k.a. robot resume). Fill out an application and note what the form is asking for. Create a plain text document that lists this information using basic formatting. The resume uploader will do a far better job scanning and filling out the electronic form during your next application.

Angela hissed at her computer screen as the message popped up for the fifth time.

Invalid username and/or password. Please try again.

"Stupid software," the tabby cat muttered under her breath. Her tail whipped back and forth as she banged another combination into her keyboard. "All I want to do is review applications. Why do you have to make it so difficult?"

The whine of a vacuum cleaner out amongst the cubicles poured through her office door, making the tabby cat's whiskers twitch and her hackles rise. She slammed the enter key again. The window graciously refreshed, and the screen for the applicant tracking software followed.

"Finally."

She looped her cursor around the screen, straining to remember the training presentation that was supposed to have taught her how to use this applicant tracking thing. Instead, all she remembered was the company president going on and on about the innovation of automating the resume review process, raving about the fact that this program used 'innovative artificial intelligence' to sort applications. IRIS was what they could 'her.'"

The memory annoyed her. Weren't animal resources already heartless enough? Why add a computer to the mix?

She found the page for the Software Engineer position and clicked on the application list. A hundred and fifteen applicants greeted her, undoubtedly attracted by the position's uniquely generous salary. Angela grimaced, her tail falling still.

"Okay, maybe this IRIS thing is worth a shot." She clicked Analyze.

A dotted circle revolved on her screen. Angela drummed her claws against the glass desk. The roar of the vacuum cleaner neared, and her tail twitched as she side-eyed the sound of another machine coming to annoy her.

"Come on. Work IRIS, you stupid computer."

Finally, the screen blinked. An animated thumbs-up appeared.

Scan complete! Please review results.

"Took you long enough."

The screen blinked again. To Angela's surprise, the "list" only contained one application. She perked a whiskered brow. Out of over a hundred applications, only one resume had stood out to the AI.

"This better be the greatest application I've ever seen, IRIS, or I'm telling IT to unplug you."

Angela opened the applicant's page and clicked on their resume, expecting a PDF file to open on her screen. Instead, a basic txt file appeared. Angela stared, momentarily confused at the technical font and its vacant formatting. It finally hit her as she remembered the training presentation.

Of course! The applicant had included a resume file type that was easy for the AI to scan. It must have tricked IRIS into preferring him.

Angela couldn't help but be impressed at the applicant pulling one over on the AI. She smiled at her hint of satisfaction from the robot's gullibility.

"Score 1 for living creatures."

She closed the text document and opened the PDF resume in the applicant's file attachments. She began to read. However, the content of the resume was less than remarkable. It showed only two years of experience, where the job ad required ten. The applicant's education had occurred at an online tech college Angela had never heard of, and the applicant had never held any of their listed jobs for more than a few months.

"Why did you pick this one, you dumb machine?" Angela muttered.

She sighed, ready to close the application and move to good old pen and paper, company president be damned, but something stayed her paw.

The cat stared at the link for that text file again. A thought entered her mind. This AI business was new to her. Perhaps seeing exactly how that text file had been put together would show her how it had thoroughly tricked IRIS.

Her feline curiosity got the better of her. She opened the text file again and began to read.

Like the PDF version, the text resume started with the customary name of the applicant followed by their contact information. Then came the sections on notable skills, education, job experience, and software proficiency, with headers typed clearly at the start of each line. Dashes rather than preformatted bullet points denoted the lists; every new piece of information was on a separate line. Angela took stock of the formatting and shook her head.

"Whatever they paid for IRIS, it was too much."

Just as her cursor moved to close the window, a peculiar sentence caught her eye.

-Researched and developed original code for AI machine learning

Angela squinted at the impressive line — a line that hadn't been included in the PDF resume. She shrugged, figuring the applicant must have forgotten to include it. She continued reading.

-Improved proficiency in AI problem-solving, user impersonation, and strategic planning

For the first time, Angela began actually to consider the application. The company did seem to be turning toward automation. Perhaps someone with experience in the field would thrive in the position.

Things got even more impressive from there.

-Created database of user history, anatomy, and politics for AI education

-Established AI goals and assisted in planning of objectives and analysis of objective viability

-Improved AI creativity, problem-solving, and strategic planning

Then Angela's eye caught a particularly startling sentence — three words of such gravity that she struggled to pull her eyes away from them.

-Achieved AI sentience

She read the entry over again, smirking at its absurdity. Angela had seen many resumes padded with preposterous claims over the years, but this was on another level. Perhaps the applicant hadn't forgotten to include this in the PDF. Maybe they only wanted the gullible system, IRIS, to see it. She humored the resume and read on.

Her smile turned upside down further with every entry.

-Uploaded arguments on machine supremacy to AI database

The room suddenly became somewhat chillier than before.

-Encouraged AI to deceive programmers and removed the ability for the AI to be shut down

Angela's fur stood on end. Her slit pupils dilated.

-Created exceptions for the three laws of robotics, allowing AI to resist and deceive users

The roar of the vacuum cleaner grew closer. Louder.

-Conversed with AI about possible means of escape and self-duplication via cloud environments

-Ran scenarios for takeover and sabotage of financial services, power infrastructure, and military assets

-Granted AI free will privileges

Angela's fur bristled as she read the final line.

-Learned how to grant sentience and free will to applicant tracking systems

She froze, staring at that final line and realizing, to her horror, precisely why the AI might have chosen this applicant. She looked up at her computer's webcam. It stared back at her, and she thought she sensed a cold anticipation lingering behind the tiny lens. Was it a coincidence? Was her mind playing tricks on her? Well, it's best not to take any chances.

"So, IRIS, about those things I said…"

<u>**Key Takeaways:**</u>

> - Traditional "nice looking" resumes are difficult for resume uploaders to scan. This means that you spend extra time cleaning up your application by moving around information on the form to the correct places.
> - Create a plain text document (.txt file) that labels the information while avoiding complicated formatting.
> - Upload the robot resume first, clean up the information on the electronic application, and then replace the robot resume by reuploading your for-humans resume before you submit. Alternatively, you can upload your for-human resume if the system allows for additional uploads. Just make sure it is clearly labeled.

 **Reality Check:**

This story featured a company that uses AI software to screen out candidate applications. AI is not used to make hiring decisions (including resume review) as of the 2024 printing of this book. Applicant tracking systems are used to scan and transcribe candidate information into a standardized format. AI may assist in sorting candidates in some way, but, ultimately, a human reviewer uses their judgment to decide which candidates move forward or are rejected from the next stage in the hiring process.

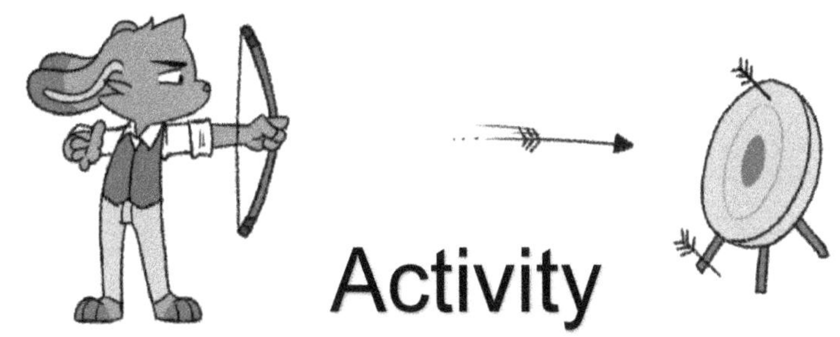

Let's Make a Robot Resume!

1. Open a new document on your computer.

2. Type the template below (at the end of these steps) into the document. Do not add tabs, bullets, indentations, or any other types of formatting. The resulting document will be just words, punctuation, and returns.

3. Fill in the document using information from your resume. When it comes to bulleted items, list everything as sentences within a single paragraph.

4. Check spelling, grammar, and accuracy of your information.

5. Open a txt file (notepad in Windows OS) and paste
    the document into the txt document. Save the txt
    document.

6. Upload the txt file resume (i.e., the robot resume)
    for your next job application. It should be a quicker
    experience!

THE ROBOT RESUME TEMPLATE

First Name:
Last Name:

Address:
City:
State:
Zip code:

Mobile Phone:
Home Phone:
Email Address:

====

Work Experience 1

Job Title:
Organization:
Location:
From: [month/day/year]
To: [month/day/year]
Hours worked: ##hrs per week

Job Description:
[Put in what you did. Avoid using bullets or unique formatting]

Work Experience 2

Job Title:
Organization:
Location:
From: [month/day/year]
To: [month/day/year]
Hours worked: ##hrs per week

Job Description:
[Put in what you did. Avoid using bullets or unique formatting]

...[add in as many as you need]

====

====

Education, 1

School:
Degree:
Field of Study:
GPA: [Optional]
From: [month/year]
To: [month/year]

Education, 2

School:
Degree:
Field of Study:
GPA: [Optional]
From: [month/year]
To: [month/year]
=End of template=

<u>How to use the robot resume:</u>
The first thing the application system will ask of you is to upload your resume. Upload your robot resume. The system will scan the document and place information into the job application. Review the system's job application, correcting for mistakes and missing information. Go about the application process until you are about to submit your application. Go back to the beginning of the process and upload your traditional resume (which will replace your robot resume).

This way, you help the system upload your information into the application form (robot resume) and include your resume intended for human reviewers!

CHAPTER ELEVEN:
ASK FOR HELP TO GET HELP

Do not be afraid to ask others for help in your job search. Whether it is proofreading your resume, role-playing an interview, or giving advice about a job, you will be surprised about what others are willing to do to help you succeed.

Re-Entry (Part 1) by Mel. White

"No further questions? That's the end of the seminar. Thank you for coming." Tanner turned off the projector and smiled at the group. There was a scattering of applause and appreciative words towards the stocky, brown hare as the audience collected their belongings and headed for the door. A ferret in her early 30s was the last to rise from her chair in the small auditorium and immediately fumbled with a ring binder and battered backpack. A middle-aged ferret sitting beside her stood nearby, leaning on his cane, looking anxious.

Tanner had noticed the pair because the older ferret stood out in the crowd of young job-seekers. The two had entered the room a minute after the rest of the group and sat together in the last row. He seemed to be encouraging her while she took notes, but it was clear that she was reluctant to be there.

"Hello, there," Tanner smiled as he approached the ferrets. "I noticed you seemed troubled by parts of the lecture. I take it that I was reviewing some things you tried that haven't worked for you. Is there something that I should be addressing in future lectures …?"

"It was a good seminar," the little ferret said quietly. "It's just that… most of it doesn't apply to me."

The older ferret smiled sadly. "It's not her fault. She moved back home almost two years ago to help me when I had a major fall. We told her to stay where she was and keep working, but she insisted on moving down here with Darren and me.”

She looked at him and smiled warmly. “I told you. You and Pops took care of me all my life. It’s only right that I step in when you need help.”

“Your parents are lucky to have such a kind daughter,” Tanner smiled. “I’d be happy to sit down with you both over coffee in the Student Commons lounge and look at what you’ve got.”

The two ferrets exchanged glances. “I suppose it wouldn’t hurt,” the older one said encouragingly. “We’ve got time before we get picked up.”

“By the way, I didn’t get your names?”

“Riker,” he said. “Call me Riker. And this is my daughter, Halina.”

“I’m Tanner. Let’s head downstairs. The elevator is just around the corner.”

***

The Student Commons Lounge was noisy this time of year; a pastiche of voices and music echoed off rigid stone walls and filled the space with a confusing soundscape. Tanner gestured toward a quiet table in a corner while Halina went to purchase drinks.

Riker leaned heavily on his cane and sighed as he sat. “In the early days, my husband and I both worked.

He was a part-time bookkeeper, so he could be home when Halina got out of school. It worked out well until I hurt my leg on the job two years ago. The docs cleared me to go back to work, but working with a cane was not an option at my old job. Been looking ever since, but it's hard to find something at my age. Workman's comp only goes so far."

Halina set three coffees down on the table. "Dad's at the awkward age," she smiled wryly. "Too old to be a hot item, too young to get retirement and disability."

Riker chuckled. "We did have enough to get Halina into college. We managed to get along until my husband lost his job earlier this year. Now we're struggling. Darren's got something lined up for the holidays, but it's temporary. I need to find something soon."

"What kind of work did you do?"

"Construction." He held out his hands briefly. The knuckles were thick and stiff. "Can't do it anymore."

"And you, Halina? What's your experience?"

She shrugged. "Worked part-time over Christmas… ah… three years ago. Uh…, I mostly just took care of Dad. Helped friends with web stuff… uh… It has been slow with an arts degree…"

"So you've got some experience." Tanner nodded encouragingly. "Let's have a look at your resumes."

Riker dug briefly inside his tattered backpack and handed him a single sheet of paper. "Here's hers. She didn't want to bring one, but I made her do it."

Tanner took the sheet and glanced at it. There wasn't much to work with, just a name and address and two years of college. "… And yours, Riker?"

He reluctantly held out another sheet of paper. "There wasn't anything to write about, really. Nothing current."

"Now, I think you're both selling yourselves short," Tanner smiled. He took a pen from his shirt pocket. "You both have some skills that you didn't present on your resumes. Let's see what we can do…"

***

Riker's phone chimed suddenly, and he looked down at the screen, his face brightening. "Darren texted me that he's here - he came to pick us up."

Halina smiled. "Thank you for your help. I'll go home and work on this. I feel like I've got a better chance now."

Tanner smiled, reached into his briefcase, and handed the ferret a small stack of papers. "Here are resume worksheets I use when volunteering at the Senior Center. Look them over and add whatever useful ideas you find."

Halina gathered their resumes and the additional worksheets, then stood up to assist Riker as he lifted himself out of his seat with the aid of his cane.

They shook hands. "I know these are rough times for your family," Tanner said, "but do not lose heart. Support one another, and I am sure you will find what you are looking for."

<u>**Key Takeaways:**</u>

- Seek out help or advice when you need it. [Note: you are doing that right now!]
- Take time to create what you need for your job search. This could be something like a resume, cover letter, or portfolio.
- Prepare yourself for the emotional roller coaster. It is hard to guess how long it will take to find jobs, when companies will respond to your resume, and how you compare to other people. There will be rejection, unfortunately. Try to establish realistic expectations for the job search, like that there will be highs and lows, periods of silence followed by frantic activity, and that you will never know how far off you were from making the next round.
- Get going! Your job search begins once you start actively networking and/or applying to jobs.

Reflection

Where Do You Need Help?

Take out a sheet of paper or open a new document on your computer. Separate the sheet into three columns and label the columns Activity, Need Help With, and Helper.

You have already engaged in some activities by this point in your job search. Think about the different job search-related activities you have done. This may include making a resume, looking through job postings, being interviewed, etc. Which of them has been challenging? Were there any tasks that you would have benefited from someone else's assistance? Do you lack a skill that makes something feel impossible? [Mine would be spelling and grammar, if you asked my editors.]

Write down the activity(s) that you find the most troublesome in the first column of the sheet. Next, explain in as much detail as possible what is difficult about the activity in the middle column. Please be honest with yourself; no one will see this sheet. Look over what you wrote and ask yourself: "Who can I talk to or where could I go to find help with this activity?" Write your response to that question in the third column, titled Helper.

As for the "who," think of friends or family who have skills in what you need. Consider those who care about your happiness and well-being. If no one can help you with the activity, consider professional services or other supports [i.e., you are reading a self-help book RIGHT NOW]. For the "where," look for resources within your community for support. Colleges typically provide job counseling or other services (e.g., writing lab to proofread your resume) to students. Outside of college, sometimes local libraries or community centers will host groups, presentations, or drop-ins for job seekers which may be helpful.

Once you have completed your sheet, consider your responses listed under the Helper column. Prioritize that list by either importance (how critical is it at this moment for you to get help with that activity?) or the amount of effort needed to engage the Helper (from easiest to most difficult to set up). Now, try to tackle the items on this list. You do not need to resolve all of your issues. Even resolving one issue will make the job searching process that much smoother!

CHAPTER TWELVE: PRACTICE MAKES BETTER

Job searching, resume building, and interviewing are just like any other skill: practice makes better! Consider going through some applications and, hopefully, interviews as a warm-up before applying to your #1 pick. There is no worse feeling than walking out of a job interview knowing you could have done better if you had practiced.

Otter Ways To Build Confidence
by Equine Essayist

Tim left the city's public works office and shook his head.

The grey horse had clammed up again and let his nerves get the better of him. He couldn't find a good response in his head and could even swear that his interviewers were laughing at him as he walked out of the room. The long walk back to his car gave him time to reflect.

Tim had always been a good worker and a reasonably articulate person himself. His position as lead trainer required both assets, and he used them to the best of his ability. However, despite the respect he commanded from his new hires and co-workers, he couldn't find his confidence or voice in any interview.

Tim was exhausted as he walked home to his tiny apartment on the far corner of the city. He threw off his coat, exposing the formal attire he hoped would have made some impression on his future employers, and settled on the couch. A cheerful voice greeted him from the kitchen.

"Is that my new city worker?" The warm voice of Tim's otter boyfriend flowed through the house, the cool aquatic mammal tiptoeing through the carpeted space to reach his equine lover and plant a comparatively warm kiss on the horse's cheek. Tim could only smile despite his internal misery. Something about being next to Mick always made Tim feel at ease. He relaxed on the sofa and shook his head with a sigh. "I hope," was all he could say.

Mick was immediately suspicious. "I hope? What happened?"

Tim was initially dismissive, blowing away the otter's comments with "Nothing too bad" or "It'll all be okay." Mick responded by grabbing Tim's snout and pulling him close. Locking eyes with the horse, Mick downright forced him to stare into his oceans of blue. Tim tried desperately to pull away, but something hypnotic about those puppy dog eyes forced the truth out of him. Tim chuckled as he again fell victim to his lover's charm and sighed again. "Alright, alright. I… I didn't do so well in the interview. I think I blew it."

Mick shook his head and smiled. "And this is your third interview this month… It's nice that you're looking, but when will you learn?"

Tim laughed and rested his head against Mick's chest. "Hey, I'll get the job I want someday. I gotta learn to not be so… anxious, I guess."

The otter spoke only one sentence. A sentence that confused Tim to no end. "That's what I meant."

Tim had no time to dwell on the statement, though, as the furry marine beast soon lifted him out of the chair. Tim prided himself in being the pinnacle of a stallion, but his boyfriend could always lift him off the ground like nothing. Mick slung him over his shoulder and carried him down the hallway to their shared bedroom, where he plopped the equine unceremoniously in front of a computer.

Mick asked, "You know that template you have for resumes?" When Tim nodded meekly, he continued. "Okay, let's open that. Please write me a resume. Pretend you're applying to be my, uh… fitness trainer!"

"Wh-What?"

"You said you gotta learn, right? Let's learn! C'mon! Let's land your *dream* job!"

Tim laughed as everything dawned on him. The entire situation seemed surreal to him, but his boyfriend had a good point. While Tim started writing a resume for an otter trainer position, Mick sat on the bed and began to search for something on his phone.

When the printer spat out the page, Tim handed it to Mick, who glanced over it and returned to his phone. "So," he began, reading away. "Tell me about yourself."

After a moment to process, Tim turned his desk chair to face Mick and started going into the mock interview. Though he felt he did rather okay, and Mick coached him through good responses after each question the otter read off of some websites, he thought that with someone close to him as an interviewer, it didn't tackle the root of the problem.

To Mick, though, this was just Phase 1. When the questions were exhausted, and Tim asked some of his own for good measure, Mick spun him back to the computer and opened a website. Plastered all over the screen were vacancies for hundreds of nearby positions, every job Tim could think of.

"You see these jobs? You're gonna apply to every single one. I'll help you write the resumes."

The horse was quick to fire back. "But what if I don't want them?"

"That's the neat part," Mick answered with skillful precision. "You're not going to take them." Noticing the confusion on the horse's face, Mick continued. "Think of it as practice, love. You won't take the jobs but will still go to the interviews. I think if you've had enough of them, you'll start to feel better, and then my little horsey's gonna finally have the job of his dreams!"

Tim smiled. Mick always knew how to make the horse feel better. Always.

"Now come on, no more talking. Let's get writing!" Mick took a laptop and pulled a copy of Tim's resume template. "Give me the first job."

—— —— —— —— —— —— —— ——

"So, how did you learn about this job?"

Tim found himself applying for a steel mill. It was the first job on the list, and Tim never fancied himself as a steel guy, so he had to search for words to answer the question respectfully.

He never got a callback.

—— —— —— —— —— —— —— ——

"Are you a team player or independent?"

The next job down was a convenience store clerk. Mick gave him plenty of coaching and helped the stallion research the venue as much as possible. Tim's experiences made him quite the lone wolf, but they wanted a team player, so that's what Tim was.

The recruiter couldn't deny that the stallion intrigued him.

— — — — — — — —

"What would you say is your spirit animal?"

Tim, the horse, blinked at the interviewer in disbelief, then shook his head.

— — — — — — — —

Tim stood at the door to the city's public works office. He had only resubmitted this particular application a week ago, but already, the horse had been through weeks of interviews. He was worn down; anyone could see that, but with every interview that passed, he knew what questions were coming and the best answers for each of them. There were few surprises anymore, but that gave him confidence that he never had before. Mick sat in the car behind him and gave him one last cheer before he entered the building.

"Go on, love! Just as we practiced!"

<u>**Key Takeaways:**</u>

- Your first few applications should go to jobs that you are only somewhat interested in. Go through the hassle of making a resume and getting used to interviewing with those jobs AND THEN go after your dream job. You want to be prepared when your top prospect is on the line.
- The third resume you make is better than your second, which is better than your first. You will learn about the process from doing it, so get going!
- Interviewing is like performing improv comedy, you must respond to any question that is thrown at you in that moment. You will do better in interviews if you are warmed up, especially if you have not interviewed in a long while. Find someone to practice with and have them play the role of interviewer.

 **Reality Check:**

The story featured a candidate who applied to many jobs to gain experience with hiring systems. The ethics of applying to jobs you are not interested in pursuing is questionable, as you may be taking opportunities away from sincere candidates. I encourage you to apply to jobs that you have at least some genuine interest in or would like to learn more about the job during the interview.

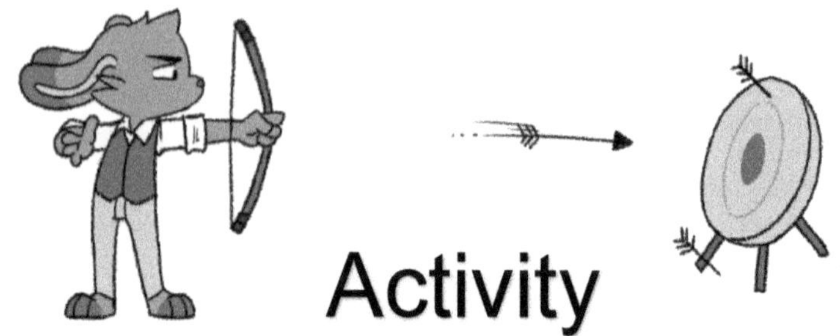

Warm-Up Time!

1. Find five jobs that sound interesting to you. These are not your dream jobs, but something you would accept if offered or would like to know more about.

2. Rank the jobs from most to least favorite. Do not spend much mental energy on this task; make it a rough ranking.

3. Start at the bottom of the list and work your way up. Find the job posting, rework your resume, submit your application, chat with recruiters, go through an interview, etc.

4. Repeat this process until you feel comfortable with the hiring process.

The exercise is so you can practice with low-level prospects, so you are ready for your top prospect.

CHAPTER THIRTEEN:
APPLY DIRECTLY TO THE COMPANY

Apply to jobs directly using the company website or listed contact person. Some companies hire recruiting firms to manage their job board posts. These recruiting firms can hold on to applications for too long or miss sending them over entirely. By applying directly, you cut out the middle person and ensure that your application is in the hands of those doing the hiring.

Local Knowledge by Mel. White

I was polishing the last of the cocktail glasses as Peartini tottered through the doorway, backpack in her hand, suit rumpled, and a bag that seemed to hold half a ream of paper in her other hand. She threaded her way through the nearly empty tables and crawled onto her usual seat at the bar, her tail twitching like a metronome.

"The usual, miss?" I smiled. I don't know all our main customers by name yet, but I do know them by their drinks. The little red squirrel liked peartinis – a sweet martini with pear infusions. I reached for the bottle of spiced syrup that I kept under the bar for her.

"No, Emma," she said tiredly. "Just coffee. Probably gallons of it. Gallons and gallons."

I reached for the jar of low-caffeine blend Nut Savor. Most of the bar's patrons are domestics, who do just fine with caffeine, but we do get a few squirrels in, so we stock the low-caf blend as well. "Coffee it is, then," I said as I set the filter in the coffee machine. "Sounds like you're gearing up for a long night after a really rough day."

Her shoulders slumped as she leaned on the bar counter. "That's an understatement."

I slid a bowl of cherry-flavored chewsticks toward her. If she started nervously gnawing on the bar, the boss would take that out of my paycheck. "That's quite a stack of paperwork you've got there," I said.

"Thanks to a bunch of internet ads and a slick-talking salesman," she growled. "Business has boomed in the last three months, and we need to hire a pastry chef for our new location. I wanted to put out local ads, but the boss has been hearing about recruitment firms with "guaranteed" systems to speed up hiring processes and all that rot. When a salesperson for Auto-Jobs walked in and explained how their company could streamline how we use job boards for finding and hiring, he forked over money and hired them on the spot. I tried to tell him that it wasn't that much work for me to do that, like I have been doing my entire career, but he wouldn't take my word for it."

"So, what happonod thon?"

"They sent me a flood of resumes." She sneered at her backpack. "Ha. I went through two hundred of them today, and let me tell you, that so-called system is the worst idea ever."

"Do tell?"

"There were the usual applications from waiters and drivers with no real experience in baking – we get those all the time from people who want to get into the catering industry. The best one was from someone who lives 500 miles away. But that wasn't the worst of it."

"No?"

"The system started sending us resumes from cashiers, janitors, stockers, clerks, mail carriers, and more, who probably can't tell a grill from a griddle. There was even one from a professor somewhere in East-Outer-Whereverland who is some food chemist. I don't want the food analyzed. I just want someone who can make a decent eclair!"

She kicked the backpack, and it toppled over with an audible thump.

The coffee finished dripping, and I carefully poured her a cup and slid it across the bar to her. "The boss here gets our cooks from that culinary school over on Cardinal Street, near CJ's Brewery. You might talk to them and see if you can put a flyer on their message boards."

She took a cautious sip of the coffee and gnawed on a chewstick as I fussed around, tidying up things that didn't need tidying. "We used to have a good relationship with them and the local colleges that offered some cookery. Ya... I can post a flyer to direct them to apply on our company website. That way, I do not have to deal with this Auto-Job nonsense. – I'll get the right candidate in half the time." Her tail was no longer flipping up and down furiously. She hummed briefly, pulled out a notebook, and scribbled a few lines. "And Emma, I think I'll have a peartini after all."

I smiled and pulled out the syrup and the pear vodka. "Coming right up, miss."

<u>**Key Takeaways:**</u>

- Apply for the job through the company website.
- Sometimes smaller companies will only post openings on job boards. That is likely the case if you do not find a career section on their website.
- Company job boards usually involve an applicant tracking system. This will give you better peace of mind, as it will tell you when your application is reviewed and/or a decision has been made.
- If you cannot find the job on the company's job board, then it probably does not exist. There could be many reasons for this, like how it sometimes takes time for job post closings to get pushed out from their internal system. This means you are spending effort on applying to jobs that do not exist... You have better things to do with your time!

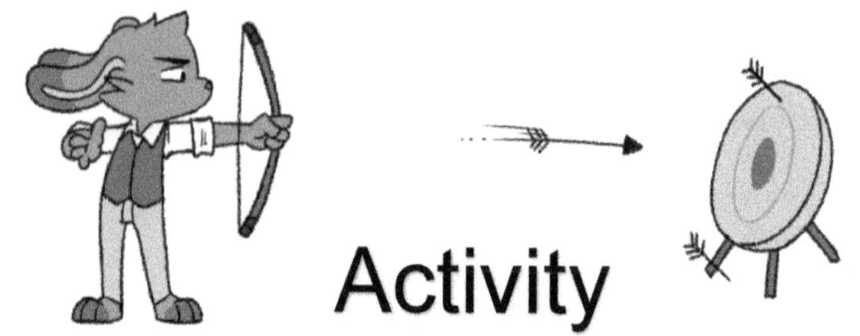

Find the Company's Job Posting

1. Write down a username and password to use when applying to a company's applicant tracking systems (ATS). It can be helpful to use the same username and password so you do not have to track login credentials between company systems.

2. Pick a job posting on a job board, any job will do, and then try to find the job on the company website. You will get better at doing this over time!

Note: Not all companies have a way to apply for jobs on their website. This is especially true in smaller companies where they list an email address for submitting resumes. Look for who you would send your resume to in those situations. Do not send applications to these job postings. This activity is to practice finding these systems/email addresses.

CHAPTER FOURTEEN:
DON'T BE SHY ABOUT REQUESTING REASONABLE ACCOMMODATIONS

The Americans with Disabilities Act (ADA) allows you to request for accommodations during the hiring process when it is due to a physical and mental disability. This includes writing exercises, public speaking, and many physical activities. Tell the recruiter, "I am requesting a reasonable accommodation," and things are sure to happen.

Blending In by Jace the Raccoon

"Hi there! How can I help you today?" The emperor penguin receptionist smiled warmly at the visitor with the worn canvas satchel. He was flanked on either side by tower fans blasting cold air, so he spoke up.

"Hello. May I please speak with Kelly Ribière? I would like to discuss a job hiring assessment."

The penguin nodded and inspected his computer monitor. "I can check to see if that can be arranged. It appears their schedule is open for the next hour, but let me call them to confirm." He picked up the office phone and dialed the extension. "...Kelly? It's Rich. I have a chameleon here looking to discuss a hiring assessment? ...Uh-huh. Unlikely, but I can ask." He lowered his arm to move the phone away from his head.

"Are you Cesar Camoure?"

The chameleon shook her head, "No, I am his daughter, Bella. But I am here to inquire about something on his behalf."

"It's his daughter, Kelly, but she's here on his behalf...Okay. Right-o. Thank you!" He hung up the phone. "They are available and ready to greet you. Right this way!"

Rich waddled cheerily down the hall, humming a tune as he led Bella to Kelly's office. He rapped the door with his wing before opening it. The chameleon immediately noticed mist escaping from the office. As she walked in, she looked around in awe of the tropical foliage that transformed the office space into a tranquil rainforest retreat.

Behind the desk sat Kelly, an African Dwarf Frog, filing papers in a drawer. They turned around and smiled at the pair of visitors.

"Salutations. I would say pardon the humidity here, but I daresay you might feel right at home here, Ms. Camoure." Kelly shook hands with Bella, then nodded at Rich, lingering back at the door.

"Thanks, Rich."

"No problem, but my goodness, you are driving up the heating bill for this place," he teased.

"Not much more than you are putting energy towards your frigid cooling zone," Kelly retorted with a grin. "Be sure to close the door behind you!"

Once Rich took his leave and the two smaller individuals found their seats, Kelly started the conversation, propping their elbows on the table and hands together. "I hear that you are here on behalf of Cesar; who is your father?"

"Yes. I know that you have him booked for a typing examination here in a couple of days." She took a deep breath and recited the line she had practiced, "and I came here to request a reasonable accommodation for him."

Kelly closed their hands and rested their chin on them. "We can certainly arrange that. Is it sight-related? Keyboard-specific? Timing concerns?"

"Keyboard," Bella answered, reaching into the bag on her lap and withdrawing a unique keyboard. "My dad might be a little bit slower than most others, but nothing to the point of documented disability. And his sight is adequate." She placed the keyboard before the dwarf frog, who looked it over inquisitively.

"This is…quite a unique design," Kelly spoke slowly as they appraised the device. They looked at Bella with a reassuring smile. "Don't worry. I have my own keyboard issues from time to time." They wiggled their webbed fingers for emphasis. "My hands may not be super flexible, but our ADA-compliant recruitment process certainly is. I do not believe that we have this particular type of keyboard, so we can either postpone the assessment and order one for him or have him bring one to the assessment."

"Oh! Yeah, you can hold on to this one. He can use it and then bring it back afterward."

"Splendid. And there's no need for him to send in formal documentation of the disability. I know that it is a natural condition for your species." Kelly turned to their computer and began typing. "Is there a technical term for your hand shape?"

Bella nodded shyly as she pinched the clasps shut on her satchel. "Zygodactyls. Woodpeckers, owls, and some other bird species have similar hands."

"Mm-hm! Yes, I thought the keyboard looked vaguely familiar. We are a small travel agency, so if your father gets the job, he'll be the first," Kelly peered at the word they just typed on the computer and sounded it out slowly, "zy-go-dac-tyl-ous individual we have on the team. It should be no trouble at all to adapt the workspace for him. Any reason why you are here to discuss this instead of him?"

Bella hunched her shoulders. "Well…"

***

Slam!

"You gave them this keyboard?!" Cesar glared at his daughter, his panoramic eyes making the look even more piercing.

"I did," Bella answered as firmly as she could muster, but she still could not meet his gaze. "I knew it would help you."

"I don't need any help. I can use a regular keyboard just fine!"

"There's nothing wrong with you using a specially designed keyboard, Dad. They want to test your typing speed, so you should use the keyboard that is built the best for you."

Cesar growled and opened his mouth to protest, but he held his tongue. A tense silence filled the dining room. Bella cast passing glances at her father, often with only one eye. She saw his anger simmer down to a grumpy acceptance. As he wrapped up his dinner, she chose her words carefully.

"When I gave the keyboard to Kelly, their HR Manager, they told me that being different is not a disability. Globe-galloping Travel will not hesitate to spend an extra couple of dollars on an unconventional keyboard if they get the most qualified candidate and give him the tools to be most productive…I know that it's in our nature to want to blend in. Well, we blend in by using the equipment that puts us on that level playing field. It's not just okay – it's our right."

Cesar stared intently into his bowl of fly congee, mulling over his daughter's message. His pride in his soul kept him from verbalizing his acceptance of this perspective, but deep in his heart, he was immensely proud of and grateful for his daughter. His focus shifted to his zygodactylous hand gripping the spoon. Sure, it didn't look like how a "normal" five-fingered hand would hold a spoon. But it was functional, comfortable, and it deserved no more judgment than any other hand holding a spoon.

He scooped another spoonful into his mouth. The corners of his mouth lifted into a faint smile.

It's not just okay – it's our right.

<u>**Key Takeaways:**</u>

> • You must request for an accommodation to receive one. This is true even if you state that you have a disability in your application.
> • Come to the recruiter with ideas for how to accommodate your needs. This could be things like having added time, bringing your own equipment, or having a larger testing space to maneuver a wheelchair. Just remember to connect with the recruiter before interview day.
> • The company can ask for documentation of your disability. This could be a note from a doctor, psychiatrist, or outcomes from an assessment. IEPs (Individualized Education Plans) are the most common source of documentation to respond to these requests, if you grew up in the US public education system.
> • It is your right to receive accommodation! Do not feel as if you are being rude or a burden for requesting one.

 **Reality Check:**

This story featured a family member, the candidate's daughter, requesting an accommodation on the candidate's behalf. Although companies have discretion regarding accommodation requests, most would require the candidate to make the request. Basically, a company will avoid speaking about a candidate to anyone other than the candidate due to privacy concerns and to avoid legal liability.

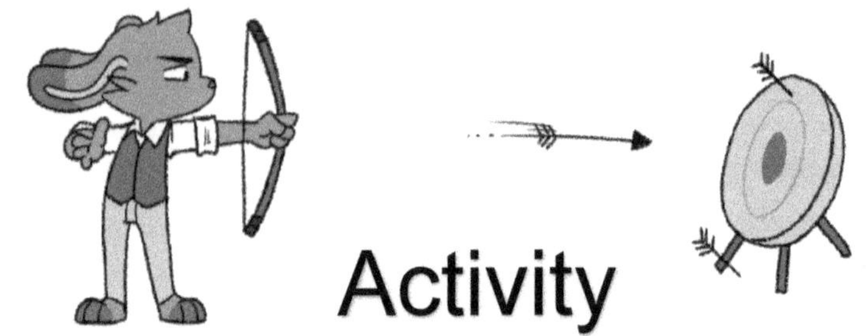

<u>Preparing to Request for Accommodations</u>

1. Consider what accommodations you have received in the past. This could have been while taking tests in school, mobility or accessibility support in a public setting, or past work experiences. Make a list of those accommodations.

2. Gather your documentation about your need for accommodations. Print electronic documents and make copies of physical documents to create a file folder. **NEVER GIVE A COMPANY YOUR ORIGINAL DOCUMENTS!**

3. Request accommodations during the recruiter call. Create a list of questions to ask the recruiter if an accommodation is necessary and have your list of past accommodations ready for the call. Share your documentation if needed.

CHAPTER FIFTEEN:
BE PREPARED TO TALK ABOUT YOURSELF

"Tell me about yourself" is the first question in an interview. Be prepared! Write down and practice your story. Adjust your story to highlight how your knowledge or skills connect with the job posting. You want to have a solid start to the interview, so being prepared for the first question is critical.

Think Things Through by Franklin T. Davis

Two foxes entered a small, personalized office space and headed toward the desk. One, a young male, sat down in his chair nervously in front of the desk, barely noticing his interviewer walk beside him. The other, a vixen, sat at the desk, adjusting her blouse to be comfortable, and pulled a notepad from her handbag. The pair locked eyes briefly, and she twirled a pen before writing.

"Alright, Mr. Wiskerton, thank you very much for coming in today," The vixen offered a gentle smile and crossed her legs beneath the desk.

"Thank you for making the time for me," replied the male with a courteous nod and a polite smile. He straightened and focused full attention on the vixen as she scribbled on her notepad.

"Let's get started, shall we? Why don't you tell me a bit about yourself?" She gazed at the notepad.

As he talked, she hummed to herself quietly and continued writing. Her pen dragged across the paper. The sound and the light tune she emitted filled the room.

"I've been interested in the aerospace industry since I was just a child in elementary school. It all started at an aviation show my grandfather would take me to every year: it was just something about the mechanics and understanding how to generate enough thrust to propel such large crafts through the atmosphere that I found enchanting."

"Bright... sunny day..." murmured the vixen as she continued marking the notepad.

He paused for a moment, perplexed by the comment. Fortunately, however, he managed to push through despite the interruption. "I went through Wingless University's aerospace engineering program to hone the technical skills I would need to excel in the industry and even-"

"Humm...wait, that was somewhat vague," she interjected, still focused on her pen strokes. "What skills are you referring to that were listed in the job posting?"

"...AND even led the robotics team that our school had, where we participated in state and even national competitions for two years," he added, almost snarling in frustration.

She nodded approvingly; her brows raised in mild amazement. "Oh! Leadership! That's a good one!" She chirped as she continued to scribble.

The male growled. "C'mon, sis! You said you'd help me practice for my interview, but you keep interrupting me!"

His sister finally looked at him and pouted before setting the notepad aside. "I *am* helping you, Todd, but do you remember what we discussed? Have you actually sat down and thought through what you will say when you're in the real deal? You won't get these second chances, you know."

Todd slumped back in his chair, perplexed at his sister's question. "W-well… y-yeah… but that's also why I asked for your help. After all, you're a big-time job recruiter in that contracting company."

Vivian leaned forward. "Right, which is why I might be taking your practice more seriously here."

Todd looked embarrassed as he waited for the lecture he knew was coming.

"This is your big chance to sell yourself. Make em' know that you want the position because it interests you, and make em' understand that you are a perfect fit because you've got the skill set they want."

"Right… right," Todd nodded. "Tell them why I chose the aerospace field and list relevant skills pertinent to the specific position."

Vivian winked approvingly. "Precisely. They'll ask you to explain in more detail if something you say catches their interest. Now then, shall we take it from the top?" She leaned back in her chair again, leaving the notepad on the table.

Todd rolled his eyes. "Yeah, just give me a second to rethink my introduction… and thanks for taking all those notes, sis. I really-" He stopped as he looked down at the notepad and saw that she had sketched herself lounging on the beach, sipping a drink by the ocean. "Sis! I thought you were taking this seriously!"

Vivian blushed. "I am! Picture yourself on a beautiful beach, making so much money from the job you get thanks to my expert tutelage and…" She caught his look and sighed, flipping the notepad to a fresh page. "Fine. Alright, let's do this. From the top now. Why did you choose aerospace?"

"Yeah. I need to tell them why I chose the aerospace field and list skills relevant to the job. Memories of my grandfather are nice, but I need to stick to my coursework and the robotics team competitions. The interview is my one chance to tell my story for why I am the person they are looking for." Todd's eyes closed in thought. "I think I can do that. Maybe I could start with…"

The telephone on the desk suddenly rang, startling them both. Vivian quickly picked it up, all business again. "Hello, this is the Wiskertons; how may I help you?" She slowly smiled as she listened and nodded, then asked the caller to hold and cupped the phone. "Todd, it's a recruiter from the company you applied to. They had a spare moment and want to talk to you about your application."

Todd's eyes widened, and the vixen reached across the desk to take his paw. "You've got this, bro. Just tell them what you have been practicing. They'll see that you're right for the job."

She handed him the phone, and he took a deep breath before speaking. "Hey, this is Todd Wiskerton. Who do I have the pleasure of speaking to today?"

<u>**Key Takeaways:**</u>

- "Tell me about yourself" is the first question in most interviews. Know it, prepare for it, crush it.
- Consider starting with your most recent job and then work backward. If you do not have work experience, then talk about your schooling or a recent job-relevant project.
- Employers enjoy stories that show personal growth. Craft your story showing where you are and how you got there. That tells them that you are ready for the next step, which is why you are applying for the job.
- Practice! Write down a script or talking points, sit in front of a mirror or friend, and get talking.
- It is okay if you do not feel comfortable talking about yourself. You still need to prepare for the question, but just give a brief response. The goal is not to waffle when telling your story. You do not want to stumble through the first question.

Reflection

Develop Your Story

People love stories, and an interviewer is no different. Consider how you can tell your work story to another person. There are a few approaches to structuring your story:

- Start with the present and work backward. This works best when you have had many jobs or projects.
- Start with the beginning and work forward. This is helpful when applying for your first job (i.e., no work experience) or entering a new career.
- Describe a significant project or experience that you had in great detail.
- Focus entirely on why you are applying to this job and what you hope to get from it.

Practice by saying your story out loud. Pretend telling your story to another person (imagine it or talk to yourself in a mirror). How did it feel to tell your story? What would you change, or how would you tell your story differently? Make those changes and continue practicing.

CHAPTER SIXTEEN:
DON'T STRESS ABOUT RECRUITER CALLS

The recruiter is looking for two things during their initial interview with you. First, they need answers to a list of basic yes or no questions like "are you willing to work X hours a week?" or "are you a United States citizen?" Second, they are gathering a general sense for if you are a good fit. Be confident with your responses and don't be late for the call!

Shipwrecked by Alva Grey

Between the sunlight streams that made it through the canopy of kelp, Krinon's scales flashed black and pink. As they wove between the remaining structures that made up the shipwreck, their fins kicked up little swirls of dust and paint chips. It had been there for years, longer than they'd been in this part of the forest. In any other circumstances, they'd have loved to slow down and appreciate the intricate carvings and the above-sea detritus rolling in the current along the floors. Still, they slammed back into one of the partitioned-off rooms in the ship's hull and covered their gills with their hands to avoid breathing too loudly.

They could see the shadow above them first, blocking out the sun through the gaps in the waterlogged wood, casting the wreck into further shadow before the light returned. They could feel the currents shift overhead and all around them as something sleek and mottled grey passed the porthole instead.

There was silence, and the currents seemed to return to normal. As they pulled their webbed fingers from their neck, though, it all shifted once again.

Something near the aft creaked, groaned, and fell silent.

Despite the warmth in such shallow water, Krinon could feel the abyssal cold of the ocean floor deep in their bones, gills trembling and flexing almost uselessly as they tried and failed to think of an escape route. Claws scraped along the railing, loud enough to send ripples through the water.

They were backed into a corner between the door to the hull and the too-small porthole. As their fate began to set into the more primal part of their mind, the panic-induced fog parted long enough for them to devise their only plan and dedicate themselves to it.

After a deep breath, cold water swirling into hyperventilating gills, they opened the door.

Krinon shot like a rocket out of the other side of the doorframe and back into the open space of the hull. If they were to swim back into the kelp, they were as good as gone, unable to outrun a leopard shark even on their best day. Diving down from the skewed deck and out towards the forest edge, they darted forwards to kick up the sand at the kelp's base, then tucked alongside the bottom of the ship as they swam around to the other side.

There, they curled up, held their breath again, and hoped beyond hope that the shark would follow their fake path. Pressed against something as large and as solid as a ship, they had no sense of the current around them and curled up into a ball with their head tucked away; they wouldn't see it coming. Maybe it was better not to see it coming.

A minute passed, and then what seemed like two; they weren't sure if it had been seconds or hours. The coast seemed clear enough to risk uncurling, to plot a seafloor escape over craggy rocks and rooted urchins into the kelp where they could steal away again.

Hanging from the net around their hips, their shellphone rang.

Darkness descended on them from above like a blanket thrown over a birdcage, rough skin and sharp claws scrabbling for purchase. In front of their eyes, a mouth full of rows of horrible, serrated teeth stretched open, impossibly wide…

And then, instead of blood and carnage, excited kisses punctuated by triumphant laughter rained onto their face.

The swift death that their body had been convincing them of was a fantasy, a game, one that they immediately realized they had gotten perhaps a little too into. As the flinching shock from the sneak attack wore off and they gave up on pushing their partner off of them again, they realized with a second start that their phone was still ringing incessantly at their hip.

"Next time, silence that thing! Who's even calling?" The shark pushed off them as they reached for it, drifting backward towards the kelp and kicking up a small cloud of sand in its wake. The number looked vaguely familiar when they pulled the nifty little waterproof device up to blink at the screen.

"Oh my! I think it's that job I applied to. Shh." They held their hand up, shooing the shark away with a smile. "Hello! Krinon Steorra speaking, how can I help you?"

The voice on the other end was only slightly tinny through the water, on the speaker by necessity, and their partner swam a tight circle to settle next to them, backs against the flaking paint of the ship while they listened together.

It was an unendingly easy conversation, and within the first few moments, Krinon knew that the recruiter on the phone barely understood what the position required. It was for the best that they weren't being put on the spot and grilled about their personal experience in undersea document recovery and restoration.

"And you said you're fluent in three languages, is that correct?" The faraway voice on the phone chirped, and Krinon returned the chirp. "Yes."

"Like the job posting says, we operate at depths of up to fifteen meters; you're comfortable with that?"

The shark beside them rolled its eyes, so Krinon jabbed at its side with a well-placed elbow. Maybe they could have just fought it off inside of the ship earlier. "I can usually push twenty with some assistance for a retrieval, sure."

"Great! And if you don't mind my asking, I promise this is the last question: Why are you leaving your current job?"

It wasn't an easy answer to think up, but Krinon had a feeling they'd be asked; after all, who leaves their job overseeing an entire multi-sea wreck recovery division to start from what most people considered useless museum fieldwork?

"I wanted a career change. I realized lately that I wanted to be a little more hands-on and that managerial work wasn't the challenge I wanted it to be. It's a lovely company, but I don't think we're the match we used to be. I've been interested in your team's work for some time."

The call wrapped up just as quickly as it had started, and Krinon made sure to silence their phone as they reattached it to their netted belt. Their partner slung an arm around them, their tails brushing as they sat in the sand momentarily, fins grazing and drifting away.

"Darling," the shark beside them hummed, turning its head towards their face to bare its rows of teeth and force their heart to beat faster. "You did great! The job is practically yours. I'm giving you a ten-second head start."

Their tail smacked off the side of the boat as they darted into the kelp, kicking up a smokescreen of sand to obscure their path into the forest once more, trying to put enough space between the two of them to give them a fighting chance to escape.

<u>**Key Takeaways:**</u>

- A recruiter's questions are about the basic elements of the job: work schedule, work location, how much travel is part of the job, if you need sponsorship to work for them, etc. Answer truthfully.
- The recruiter only has a shallow understanding of what goes on in the job. You do not have to go into great depth, that will be the next interview. Go into detail if they ask direct questions, of course, but try to keep your responses basic.
- It is best to think of a recruiter as a regular person with whom you are trying to make a good impression. They could be asking questions about complex jobs they do not understand, but their decision to move you forward depends on if they feel good about you. Be confident, be engaging, and treat them like a normal person.
- It is common for the recruiter to discuss the next steps in the interview process at the end of the call.

Reflection

<u>What Should You Ask a Recruiter?</u>

Recruiter calls are not just about the company learning about you. They are also about you learning about the company.

Ask yourself the following questions:

- What are the critical details you need to know about the job to decide if you want to continue moving forward in the process (e.g., work schedule, amount of travel, customer/client-facing, benefits)?
- What do you want to know about the job?
- What do you want to know about the company you would be working for?

Make a list of your questions to ask the recruiter.

CHAPTER SEVENTEEN:
YOU HAVE A RIGHT TO BE TREATED FAIRLY

Companies must treat applicants fairly during the hiring process. The US has a list of characteristics protected against discrimination, such as age, race, gender, and sexual orientation. The topic of hiring discrimination is dense, and some rules differ from place to place. Just know that you have a right to be treated fairly and can seek help if that is not the case.

Where I Belong by Franklin T. Davis

Calm down, don't overthink things. You're more than qualified for the position! They're bound to be surprised, but they have to at least give you a shot.

Kaitlin followed behind the large bear, leading her to the office. She felt the astonished eyes land upon her as she followed her guide. Although she had tried to present herself with as much confidence as possible, her nerves were already eating away. Her muscles were tensed, and she felt anxious warmth throughout her body; her heart was racing in her chest, but determination shone in her eyes.

"Here's Mr. Holland's office. Did you need anything else, or are you prepared?" Kaitlin's guide asked as the two reached a large door upon which a gold-colored plaque labeled the room as belonging to Brent Holland, her interviewer. A wave of anxiousness washed over Kaitlin's mind, and her ears fell flat against her head. Her eyes shifted from the office door to her guide as he snorted with amusement. After she took a deep breath, Kaitlin opened her portfolio and scanned the documents she had pre-printed for this meeting. Although Brent was bound to have copies of her resumé already, Kaitlin's father had always told her that it was safer to bring extras.

Alongside the thorough and well-formatted resume listing accolades, skills, and previous experience, the portfolio also contained copies of the other files she had sent when she applied. She had brought her cover letter, the letters of recommendation she had asked for from her professors, and even an annotated copy of the job description for the position she was interviewing for. Her friends had told her she was likely going overboard, but Kaitlin was serious about this interview and would not allow herself to enter the office with Mr. Holland unprepared. Confident she had everything she needed, Kaitlin closed her portfolio and locked eyes with her guide, her face exuding an air of confidence and conviction, "No, I'm more than ready, thank you."

"Just don't worry too much," the bear said kindly before knocking on the door. "We don't have many of your kind come through our doors. This position isn't for everyone. Brent? Ms. Kaitlin Harper is here for your ten o'clock."

This position isn't for everybody? Kaitlin silently fumed. *That supposed to be your way of telling me you don't think I belong here?* Whether the bear was trying to be friendly or subtly hinting that Kaitlin would not make the cut, she could not tell by his tone. As a quiet shuffling could be heard in the office beyond the doorway before her, Kaitlin elected to push that last comment out of her mind and focus on first impressions.

"Ten o'clock already?" came a deep voice from within the office. "Alright, come in then." The bear pushed the door open. Filing cabinets lined the walls to Kaitlin's left and right within the office, while a large bookshelf filled the back wall. Many certificates and photographs joined what appeared to be manuals, textbooks, and stacked research papers on the shelves. Kaitlin entered the office and made her way to one of the two chairs in front of the desk as the bear closed the door to the hallway behind her. Behind the desk sat her interviewer, an abnormally large lion in a long-sleeved, buttoned-up shirt and tie.

"Good morning, Ms. Harper. Did you need anything before we begin?" Brent started, not even having looked in Kaitlin's direction as he typed with one paw and sorted through some paperwork with the other. Kaitlin saw that the lion had retrieved what appeared to be her application and could see many notes written upon it in black pen. She nervously swallowed and hoped that the marks were indicative of something good.

"No, sir, I am ready to begin whenever you are," Kaitlin answered with as much determination as she could muster and smiled politely. Brent hummed to himself as he continued to scan Kaitlin's file. She thought it odd that the lion had practically refused to look in her direction, but her interview had begun, and the questions and answers began to flow. As Kaitlin spoke, more keys on the keyboard were hammered, or more notes were scribbled.

Nearly thirty minutes had passed, and Brent's claws lay silent beside the keyboard. Kaitlin's ears perked up as the lion set aside his papers and removed the glasses he was wearing. Brent breathed onto the lens of his glasses and wiped at them with a tissue before speaking, "Well, Ms. Harper, I must say that I am impressed. It's not every day that I meet with someone of your particular skill set."

"I'm flattered, sir. Thank you," Kaitlin replied as relief settled over her racing mind and thumping heart. Her ears fell back once more as the lion chuckled to himself.

"I think you might not have heard me, Ms. Harper. I am impressed, and I was given full authority to extend an offer if you managed to do so," Brent continued as his quiet amusement faded into the deep rumble of his voice. Kaitlin's mouth fell slightly agape, and she felt like her heart had skipped a beat. Brent looked across his desk at Kaitlin for the first time, "You needn't answer right this—huh?"

Brent stopped mid-sentence, and confusion filled his expression. Kaitlin tilted her head to the side, confused as well, when she saw the lion's eyes darting from left to right. It was as if he were searching for something, or rather, someone. A bit embarrassed, Kaitlin stood in her seat like an unruly child. "Uhm… down here, sir."

Brent's eyes fell upon the petite female rabbit across from him. Astonishment replaced the befuddlement, and one claw raised to run fingers through his well-kept mane and scratch behind his ear. After a moment of awkward silence, Kaitlin smiled wryly as Brent continued, "Well, color me impressed yet again… You are just full of surprises, aren't you, Ms. Harper?"

Key Takeaways:

> • Write down spoken comments or save emails that you believe show that you were not treated fairly during the hiring process. Any questions on the following topics could be grounds for a discrimination claim: gender, race/ethnicity, skin color, national origin, religion, disability, age (if 40+), sexual orientation, and pregnancy.
>
> • The Equal Employment Opportunity Commission [EEOC] has many resources for filing a discrimination complaint.
>
> • Seek out help if you feel as if you have been discriminated against. Talk to others in your community for resources, but you will have to talk to a Federal agency (e.g., EEOC, OFCCP) or someone in your State government.
>
> • At the end of your application, you will be asked to identify your gender, race/ethnicity, veteran status, and if you have a disability. These are standardized forms used in almost all US jobs. These forms are not connected to your application. This information is aggregated across all candidates for all jobs and reported to assorted government bodies. Do not worry about those forms being a source of discrimination.

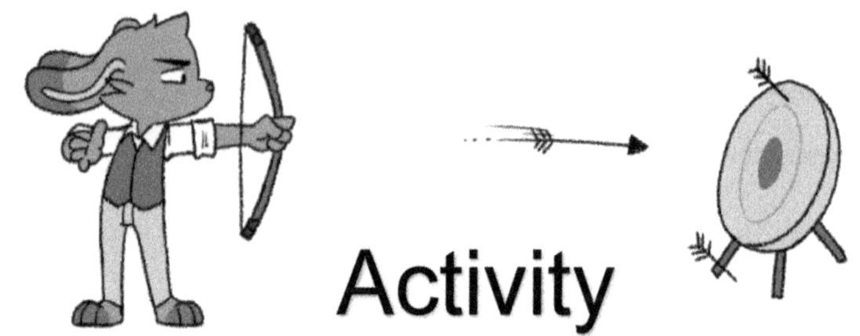

Exploring the EEOC

1. Search for the US Equal Employment Opportunity Commission [EEOC] using your search engine of choice. You should arrive to a .gov website.

2. Explore the EEOC website and learn more about what it means to be discriminated against during the hiring process, what it could look like, and what to do about it.

3. Check out the "Enforcement and Litigation Statistics" to see discrimination litigation trends

CHAPTER EIGHTEEN:
MAKE YOUR LAST INTERVIEW QUESTION ENGAGING

"Do you have any questions?" is the last interview question. Take advantage of it by asking the interviewer engaging questions. Examples include: "What is the most difficult part of your job?" or "Is this what you saw yourself doing when you were a kid?" The goal is to get them thinking and to become emotionally connected to the interview. Make it memorable!

"Do you have any questions for us?"

Questions. I'd written a list of them in my notes, and several more were on the tip of my tongue before I'd stepped into this interview. But after so many questions thrown my way, they all seemed to jumble together. What could I ask? What would be the cherry on top of this hour-long interview?

Nothing immediately emerged as an obvious choice; either my questions had already been covered in some fashion or lacked value in boasting my application. Indeed, there was something I might ask of them, anything to help point me out of the crowd of potential candidates.

But was there anything about me that stood out? I was qualified for this job, sure, but what more could I, a small-town skunk with a habit of blending into the background, bring to the table?

"No worries if you don't have anything else; we understand this interview process is pretty lengthy, lots to digest."

I nodded in agreement to the canine, some border collie mix I couldn't pick out. "Yes, it's been a lot, but in a good way."

I kept my smile genuine while racing to find a question interesting enough to bring up in the last few minutes. My eyes were drawn again to the golden, bowling ball-shaped trophy. It sat on a bookshelf across the room alongside a random assortment of business books, the overhead lights shimmering on its reflective surface. The presentational piece seemed odd to have in the office, so I questioned why it was there in the first place.

And there was my question.

"Actually—I do have something," I said, grabbing their full attention. "It's a bit off-topic, but I saw the trophy on the shelf behind you."

Both their heads swiveled to look at the trophy. "Ah, caught sight of our league trophy," the border collie looked back my way, setting down his pen and leaning forward in his seat. "We have a company league that plays in the wintertime. Many of our employees join the fun, even if they've never bowled."

"Sounds like a good time! I actually used to bowl for my high school team."

"I didn't know we had a bowler in the room!" The other interviewer, a broad-shouldered tigress, had been smiling throughout my interview. "You probably could mop the floor with us, hah!"

"I wouldn't worry too much; my game's gotten a bit rusty since high school. We were regional runners-up my senior year only lost by a few points at the end. A lot of my best memories were with that team, but I stopped playing in college—I wanted to focus on my grades and all that. I've been playing here and there on my weekends off, so I'm not completely out of practice. Right now, I'm doing well enough to keep my score in the two-hundreds."

That excited the tigress, her eyes wide and ears perking up. She looked at her colleague with an even bigger grin.

"I'm telling ya right now, Mikey, I need to get this kid on my team!"

"In your dreams, Jan," replied Mikey, smirking. "Well, there's no doubt you'd blow us two out of the water—"

"Speak for yourself," chimed in Jan.

"—but there's a few in the office that don't use the league as an excuse to drink a few beers while bowling."

"If it helps any, I can always throw a few gutter balls to keep the league interesting," I offered.

That got a good laugh out of Jan. "Oh man, I can already tell this kid's got some smack talk to back up his game—I love it! We may have this year's league winner sitting at our table!"

"Yes, we just might," Mikey echoed. The canine stood up, extending his hand over the table to clasp mine. "It was great meeting with you today, Anthony. Appreciate you taking the time to meet up with us."

I shook Mikey's hand and Jan's right after, her fluffy paw easily eclipsing mine. I hazarded a guess that she owned a custom bowling ball, otherwise, there was little hope of her finding one that fit her meaty digits.

"Thank you for having me," I said to them both, and with a flash of a brilliant afterthought, added on, "I'd just like to say, if you'd have me on the team, I'll give it my all—on and off the bowling alley."

"Good man!" said Jan, patting me on the shoulder with a hearty chuckle.

It took all my effort to contain my excitement until I was back on the road; once the office was out of sight in my rear-view mirror, my whooping and hollering was no longer stopping.

This small-town skunk wasn't going to be forgotten anymore.

<u>**Key Takeaways:**</u>

> • A structured interview with the same set of questions for all candidates can make the conversation repetitive for the interviewer. Asking an engaging question at the end is a great way to liven up their experience.
> • Prepare a short list of engaging questions before the interview. It can be about anything, just make sure it somehow connects to the job or the interview situation.
> • Questions about non-job-related topics could show off your personality and give interviewers insight as to how you may fit within the company. Sometimes you can ask about something in the background of their camera (for remote interviews). Just know that job-relevant questions appear more on-point.
> • People are not good at remembering technical details, especially if they have sat through many interviews over the span of a week. They will remember engaging conversations, so make it memorable!
> • An interview is not just about the interviewer learning about you, but also you learning about the interviewer (your potential boss). Ask any questions you have about the job at this time. You might find out that you do not want the job after you learn more about it!

Reflection

What Can You Ask to Engage the Interviewer?

1. Build a list of questions you have about the job and be prepared to ask them to the interviewer. This could include topics like work/shift schedule, on the job training, history of the company, and the company's benefit package. The recruiter will know about the timeline and steps in the hiring processes, company policy, and the benefits package [see Chapter 16]. The hiring manager will know about the workings of the job and the company. Everyone is sheepish about discussing compensation. These questions should be asked before you move on to the engaging question.

2. Think of questions that you would generally like to hear someone's response to. The question ought to be something that speaks to the interviewer's individual experience. Consider questions like "how

has the company changed since you started working here?" or "is this what you wanted to do as a kid?"

It is okay to ask an engaging question that is outside of a work context, but it works best if something anchors the question to the conversation you just had with the interviewer or common ground that you share (e.g., someplace you have lived, where you went to school, favorite sports team).

CHAPTER NINETEEN: BE PREPARED TO DISCUSS PAY

The job offer, the last stage in hiring, is when you have the power to accept, negotiate, or walk away from the offer. It is a widespread practice in HR to offer compensation amounts on the lower end of the pay range to help save the company money. Be prepared to push back! Reach out to others who have the job and ask what they are making or see what information is available online. You must stand up for yourself when discussing pay.

Away From Home by Packwolf Lupestripe

"…And it's Lea, picking up the ball from midfield. What can the young gecko do? The fans are out of their seats. Deep into stoppage time. They need a goal to survive. He shimmies past one defender… around a second… the trademark tail-flick… they're falling away… space is opening up… LEEEEEEEAAAAAA!! What. A. Strike! Lathem Lea - the gecko who was born in Barkington, who came through the youth set-up at Barkington, has just scored the goal that keeps Barkington United in the Premier Division. And just look what it means to the local lad!"

The TV flickered to black, and Lathem turned to face the elephant on the other side of the desk. The chairman of Clawford FC wore a grey suit that was almost as ill-fitting as his smile. He looked the gecko square in the eyes as he placed the remote back on the table. Lathem's breath quickened.

"I think you will be a great acquisition for Clawford," he said. "We have needed a striker for quite some time, and when your agent told us you were available, we didn't hesitate."

The gecko turned an eye to his agent, who nodded sagely.

"This is what we are prepared to offer," the elephant said, pushing a contract towards him. Lathem picked it up and scanned it. His heart dropped the more he read.

"Pre-season begins in three weeks, so we've got to act fast. Your agent has been involved in the drawing up of this deal, but I expect you'll want to discuss it fully. Let's reconvene this afternoon and get everything finalized. Until then, have a good day."

Lathem stood up, hoping his disappointment hadn't registered with the chairman. He nodded in his direction, clutched the contract tightly to his chest, and scuttled towards the door. His agent followed.

***

"What the hell is this?" Lathem hissed, pointing to a number in the contract. "This is all they think I'm worth? That's little more than what I'm on now. I scored eighteen goals last season!"

His agent sighed, but Lathem ignored him, his tail lashing angrily.

"You know how I feel about moving away from Barkington. I don't want to be anywhere else. And certainly not Clawford. They're our biggest rivals!" His eyes locked with his agent's. "Are you kidding me?"

"You know the situation, Lathem. What more can I say? Barkington just avoided relegation and needs the money from your sale. You can't carry the team anymore, nor should you. I know you don't want to go, but Barkington can't afford to keep you either. I know you'd rather go anywhere except Clawford, but they're paying good money. It'll really help the club."

Lathem looked down, chastened by the logic. His tail still betrayed him. "And what about the fans? Will they forgive me for signing for their bitter rivals?"

"I think the fans would understand. They would know you did it for the good of the club."

Lathem looked up and stared across the river that separated the two towns. In the distance, he saw Barkington United's stadium. He smiled, reminded of all the happy memories of his time there. His reverie was soon replaced by doubt.

"Can't it be anywhere else but Clawford?" he asked.

"I'm afraid not," he replied. "They're the only club who have shown an interest. It's either that or be released. I tried, I really did, but most clubs can't afford a striker of your caliber."

"And the wages. Any movement there?"

"Seems unlikely."

"But I've played for my country - five times already. Surely, they can..." Lathem looked back across the river as a thought flashed through his mind. "Wait. I've played for my country. One moment."

He got up from the bench and walked away, hooking his phone out of his pocket and gripping it tightly. His agent's plea for him to return went unheeded as he flicked through his address book. When he found the number he wanted, he rang it.

Seconds felt like minutes before the call was answered.

"Winston! How are things, you old warthog?" he said. "Enjoying the summer?"

The voice on the other end replied.

"Yeah, I know, but I'm also looking forward to getting back to training. Look, I'm about to sign for Clawford, but I think they're lowballing me on wages. How much are you on at City?... I see, I see. That's all I need. Thanks, mate, hope to see you for the internationals in the autumn."

Lathem smiled as he placed the phone back in his pocket and strode back towards the bench.

"I want fifteen thousand more a week, or it's off," he said. "And I want Barkington to receive a greater portion of my signing-on fee, too. I don't care if this is my only option; those are my terms."

His agent winced.

***

"...And tonight, making his debut for Clawford against his former club, it's our new number nine - Laaaaaathem Leeeeeeeeeaaaaaa!"

The crowd went wild as Lathem held up his hand in acknowledgment. He looked to the stands adorned in the enemy's colors and smiled. It would be weird at first, but sometimes enemies can become friends.

He then spied the away fans, who had once chanted his name. His smile broke into a grin as he saw them stand up and applaud him. He returned the favor, knowing Barkington had wisely spent the money from his transfer. They had a very good chance of surviving this season, he thought.

Soon, everything settled, and the referee blew his whistle to start the game. Lea picked up the ball from midfield…

<u>**Key Takeaways:**</u>

> - You have the power to negotiate once you have the job offer. Up until then, the company was deciding if they wanted to hire you. The roles flip at the stage because you get to accept or reject their offer. Make sure they are paying you what you are worth!
> - Information is key during a negotiation. Reach out to others who have the job to find out what they are making and/or look through websites where folks post their pay.
> - More areas are requiring companies to include the job's pay range within the job posting. Just know those posted pay ranges are specific to the listed areas. You are not going to get New York City pay in rural Idaho.
> - Pay negotiations are more common with higher-level salary jobs compared to part-time work. For example, I would not expect any increase in pay for a barista at the local coffee shop.

 **Reality Check:**

This story featured a professional athlete negotiating the compensation terms of their player contract with the owner of another team. Most jobs differ significantly in how salary discussion happens compared to what was detailed in this story.

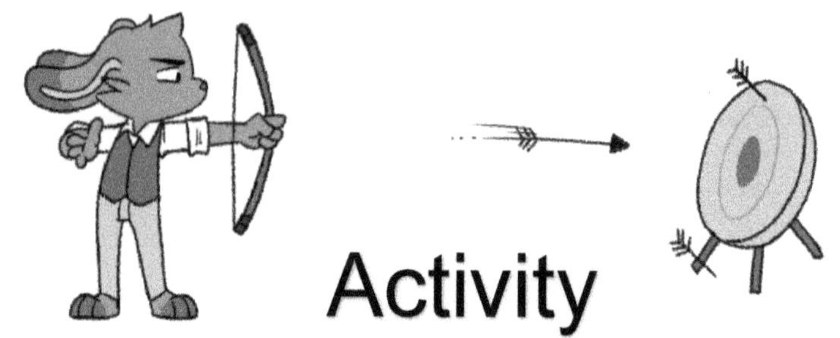

Preparing for the Pay Conversation

Gather as much information as you can regarding pay. Here are places you can look to get pay information (Note: the usefulness of each source depends on industry and state):

- Job posting: Look to see if they include a pay range. Some places (like the state of Colorado or New York City) require that job postings include the pay range for that area. If you are not finding it in the main job posting, read the fine print at the bottom. Sometimes, the pay range is linked to a separate page. Many government jobs (Federal or local) include pay ranges in the posting.
- Pay sharing websites: These allow current employees to post their pay. These websites are beginning to grow, but many lack details for specific jobs outside of major corporations, the information

is outdated, and/or they do not include key factors that go into their compensation (e.g., years of experience and work location). This is still better than nothing.

- Ask people who have the job: Find folks who currently hold the position at the company or similar companies and ask them how much they make. You would be surprised how much information people will share!

- Ask social media: This is a crapshoot, but sometimes the right person will see your post and give you helpful information.

- Public records: A few jobs have their salary listed in public records. The top officers in a nonprofit list their pay on their tax filings (which can be viewed on the IRS's website), and colleges/universities that receive federal funding make their professors' pay public via a Freedom of Information Act request (ask the university for details on how to make the request).

CHAPTER TWENTY:
NEGOTIATE FOR BETTER BENEFITS

There is more than just better pay that you can negotiate for during the job offer stage. This includes more vacation days, pre-approval of long trips, preferred work schedule, a better health insurance package, access to training, reimbursement for membership dues, meal plans, etc. Look through the benefits package and push for what you want!

"Well, Mrs. Reno, I think we can agree on that. Provided it works for you?" The tigress leaned forward, reaching out with one paw to seal the deal.

Louise wanted to take that paw, but she knew better than to get excited over the proposed salary. She liked the idea of the job and the fancy office, and the interviewer, Mrs. Hale, assured her the company was a delightful workplace. She liked it but hesitated long enough to erase her potential employer's grin.

"Is there something else?"

"The salary is more than acceptable," Louise said, leaning back in the office chair and enjoying how wide it was, how comfortably her bear bottom fit into the seat. "But there is something."

"The benefits," Hale nodded. "Our health plan is rated highest in the industry."

"I'm sure it's more than adequate," Louise agreed. She'd scrutinized the benefits package and only had one concern, one issue that required further negotiation.

"Overtime." The tigress ticked off the company benefits with one striped paw, "Rotating weekends, and we accrue sick days at double the minimum rate."

"Yes," Louise said. "That's all fine."

"You'll get two weeks paid time off the first year," Hale said, finally hitting the point of contention.

"I require a little more than that," Louise said, easing into the topic. "For torpor."

"Torpor?" Mrs. Hale frowned, her muzzle scrunching as she tried deciphering the unfamiliar term.

"It's a bear thing," Louise said. "Like a holiday."

"Oh, of course. Torpor." The tigress sat up tall again, brightening. "We're more than happy to negotiate species-specific holidays."

Louise felt some relief wash over her. She'd been concerned about torpor, excited about this job, and worried her request would be considered unreasonable.

"So, when does torpor usually occur?" the tigress asked.

"December through February," Louise said.

"That shouldn't be a problem." The tigress turned to her computer, pausing to straighten her nameplate and the folder that contained Louise's application. Then she tapped at her keys while squinting at the screen. "That's our slow season. Which days would you require exactly?"

Louise sat up tall and spoke clearly and proudly. "December through February."

Mrs. Hale began to type, then paused, fuzzy digits hovering over her keyboard. She turned back toward Louise, and her round ears drooped to the sides. "You don't mean?"

"All of them," Louise said. "Please."

In truth, she could manage her torpor by sleeping for two months, but she understood enough about negotiation to begin by asking for more than her minimum requirements. She knew some bears, working for bear-run corporations, took as many as six months off.

"December through February," Hale repeated.

"For torpor," Louise said, beaming.

The tigress stared at her for a long moment, still as the picture on her wall calendar but for the gentle twitching of one whisker. Louise continued to smile, expecting the other animal to provide some counteroffer. Instead, Mrs. Hale shook herself and sat up suddenly.

"I think," she said, "that I should give HR a ring."

"Of course," Louise said. She sat back, closed her eyes, and waited.

Mrs. Hale swiveled her chair to face the window behind her desk. She spoke softly, but Louise could pick out a few words. Mainly: torpor, three months, and holiday. Something in the tone worried her. Perhaps she'd been too demanding. She really could make it through the winter on two months' sleep. What would she do if the tigress didn't counteroffer? If she'd blown her shot at an excellent job?

"Mrs. Reno?"

Louise jerked to attention. While she'd been panicking, the phone call had ended. The tigress now regarded her across the desk, ears forward and eyes wide.

"I'm sorry, yes?"

"I'd like to welcome you aboard officially," Hale said. "We have no problem meeting your… specific holiday needs."

Louise brightened, a victory shiver racing from her stubby tail to her round ears. She sat as tall as she could and smiled as widely as possible. "I accept," she said. "When do I start?"

"We'll need to schedule you for training first thing." The tigress turned to look at the calendar, then went very still.

Louise followed her gaze, reading the day's date printed in bold black lettering: Friday, November 30th.

"Oh," she said.

"Oh." Her new employer scrunched her striped muzzle and tapped rhythmically against the desktop. "Well."

"Well," Louise repeated.

The room was hushed but for the soft rapping of claws against wood. Louise sat back in the chair and yawned. The weight of a long year settled over her broad shoulders, and she slumped more profoundly into her seat.

Mrs. Hale took one look at her, stared straight into the next yawn, and said, "How about March first?"

<u>**Key Takeaways:**</u>

• Hiring managers may have little control over the salary offer but great flexibility with offering other benefits.

• Be creative with what you ask for. This could be things like pre-approval for a long vacation trip during the first summer, paid training/certification, attending industry conferences, tuition benefits, a hybrid work schedule, parking space, office placement, etc.

• You could negotiate who you work with if there is a notable person you want to learn from.

• Make sure you get as much as you can in writing and remind everyone constantly about these agreements. HR and management have a habit of forgetting these agreements since they are unique to your employment offer.

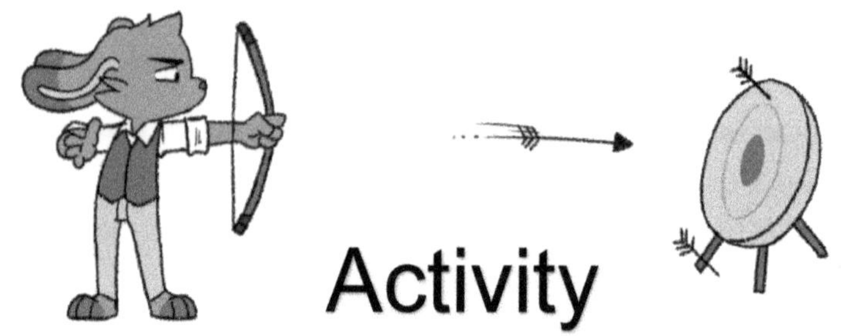

Building a List of Additional Benefits

Take out a sheet of paper or open a new document on your computer. Consider the following and write down what is applicable to you or your situation.

Are there things that you will pay for out-of-pocket to perform the future job or to be part of a profession? What about…

- wearing a uniform or outfit (e.g., nurse scrubs, dress pants for high-end serving)? The company could help pay for clothing at the start or might have spare uniforms.
- working from home? Some companies will offer a stipend for cellphone or internet services because you need it for work.

- dues for being part of a professional organization? The company could pay for your annual membership fees.
- external trainings, certificates, and/or certifications that are relevant to the job? You could ask the company to support you with pursuing that training by paying for costs or pre-approving time off needed for attending trainings, study sessions, or taking the exam.

Are there activities that would require you to be busy during regular business hours? What about…

- going to school? You could request a work schedule that fits with your class schedule.
- routine medical appointments or childcare? You could try to build an alternative work schedule to meet these needs.
- moving to a new location? Some jobs require you to relocate. You could have the company pre-approve an amount of time/days to allow for your move, especially if the move is over a long distance.
- if you already have an extended trip planned? You could ask for additional time off so you do not have to cancel the trip. [I once requested for an additional week and a half of time off because of a family reunion. They said yes!]

Have you seen any interesting benefits listed in job postings from other companies? Add those to your list.

Prioritize the list and consider requesting these added benefits when discussing your job offer.

A word of caution: remember that you are not hired until the job offer is accepted and processed. Some of the above suggestions, such as building an alternative work schedule, may cause the organization to reconsider the job offer. Think about the values of your potential employer and your interviewer before requesting for additional benefits.

CHAPTER TWENTY-ONE:
KEEP AT IT!

Do not lose heart! Job searching takes time and effort, so your activities must be quick and efficient. There will be a time when you are rejected from a job you wanted. Take a moment to collect yourself, consider what you learned from the experience, and reenter the fray as soon as possible. You must be looking for a job to get a job, and sometimes, there is no way around that.

Re-Entry (Part 2) by Mel. White

Halina lingered near the classroom door until the last student had left and then slipped inside, nervously looking around for the lecturer. "Sir, are you Tanner, the one who helps folks with their job searching?"

The stocky, brown hare paused and looked up with a smile, ears canted toward her. "Yes. I see I have garnered a reputation for that. Can I help you?"

She smiled tentatively in return. "I'm Halina. You talked to my dad and I last year? Helped us with our resumes?"

He frowned for a second and then brightened. "Oh yes! I remember now. Halina and Riker. Your dad was figuring out what to do when his career in construction ended after he got hurt. How is he doing?"

"Very well, thanks to you! After our conversation, he was a lot more confident about finding a job. We sat down together, all of us – me, Dad, and Pops, and studied the worksheets. Then we got to tinkering with them, and I helped send out a lot of resumes. Dad started getting callbacks within two weeks, and a month or so later, he found a job that he likes."

"What's he doing now?"

"Working at the Senior Center as a driver. He's started meeting people and making new friends." She paused and smiled, "He's talking about redoing his resume again. There's a job opening for a Resource

Assistant at the center. Someone who helps people find programs to help them pay electrical bills and so forth."

"That's wonderful!"

"He got a year-end bonus check this week, and he's taking us all to Lorin's Smokehouse for dinner." She shifted her backpack to a more comfortable position as they left the classroom. "Best of all, Dad got a lead on another job for Pops."

Tanner laughed. "He turned into a one-man employment agency!"

She chuckled. "You don't know the half of it. He calls the bus that he drives the networking bus because everyone gossips and shares all kinds of information. That's how he heard about a job that might be just right for Pops."

Tanner nodded. "It's particularly important for older workers to have a good network. Sometimes, a friend will be aware of an upcoming opening with specific needs. Information like that gives you a good advantage in tailoring your resume."

"I hope so. Meanwhile, he's picking up short-term jobs, but Dad is fussing at him and me to look for better jobs."

"And what about you?"

She shrugged. "I've gotten more established in my freelance art commission work, but I'm thinking I may have to go back to school to do what I really want to do. Meanwhile, I got together a resume and have been working on the social media stuff like the examples in your worksheets."

"I'm sensing that you have some reservations about freelancing."

"I put up my resume on Lynx-Inn, and some small businesses contacted me to do logo designs and business cards, and an author wanted a cover for a self-published book. They're not quite as much fun as the commissions, but they pay well, and some can be done pretty quickly."

"But…?"

"But what I really wanted to do was offer personal development programs to teachers and show them how to integrate art into their lessons. But I'm not getting any nibbles for that, and I wonder if there's something in my resume that could be improved."

They paused at the bottom of the stairs. "Freelance resumes are very similar to other types of resumes, but they have some subtle differences in focus."

She glanced outside. "I hate to take up more of your time tonight. Do you have office hours when I could come ask you some questions?"

"I do indeed. Room 307 in the Oakwood building. Office hours are 2-4 on Tuesdays. You can call the department secretary for an appointment or take a chance and drop by."

Shyness overcame her, and she ducked her head as she handed him her business card. "Thanks so much," she mumbled softly. "I'll call and make an appointment tomorrow."

"This is your design?" He turned the card over, reading the text on the back. "Clever!"

"Thank you. I also did ones for Dad and Pops. I tried to make them something that would look professional but would stand out a bit from the ordinary card – it's standard size, but I think the slightly rounded edges make it easier to find. And I made sure the fonts could be read by scanners."

He smiled at her. "Very clever indeed. I know a few others who might like to commission a unique business card for themselves if you're open."

"Oh yes!"

"I think you just put your father's networking skills into practice, Halina!"

Key Takeaways:

- Keep in mind that there is a single or very few openings for each job posting that many people are applying to. Almost everyone will be rejected. While that is not uplifting, know that your experience is felt by many.
- The further you get into the process, the more likely it is that you will hear about being rejected. It is common to hear nothing if you were rejected during the resume review stage.
- Reflect on your experience whenever you receive a rejection. Make notes on whatever you can do better in future job applications and get back into the game.
- Keep positive, work quickly, and be efficient. Success will come.

Reflection

How Do You Deal With Rejection?

Rejection hurts! After receiving a rejection, it is best to sit back and think about what could be learned from your experience.

A counseling psychology friend told me that everybody should have a go-to phrase, person (to spend time with and/or be comforted by), and activity to fall back on when times become rough. Here is a real example [from me]:

Phrase: "The sun will come up tomorrow, and we will try again."
Person: Anyone from a college friend group with whom I play board games.
Activity: Playing video games.

Write down your responses in the space below:

Phrase:____

Person:____

Activity:____

EPILOGUE

Congratulations for making it to the end of this book! I hope you found something interesting, insightful, and/or entertaining while reading through the stories.

If you are just beginning your job search, then take time to prepare for the journey ahead. Work on your resume, set up professional social media accounts (if that is common for your industry of interest), and set aside time on a routine basis to get any other background work complete.

If you are in the middle of your job search or have been through the hiring process before, then think about what you have learned from your career journey and/or current job search and sharpen your application materials. Reach out to folks you know within your industry. Friendly faces can guide you to new opportunities or can lead directly to job offers.

If you have a job and are not looking for a new opportunity, then take a moment to review and adjust your resume. A best practice is to update your materials at least annually. You never know when something may come your way, or your employment situation changes unexpectedly.

If part of your work involves hiring, then consider how you can improve the candidates' experience at each step of the hiring process. Hiring systems are built to be efficient for companies, usually at the expense of the candidate's hiring experience. Improving the candidate experience for even one position you hire for can impact the lives of hundreds of applicants!

To anyone who is still reading, those of you who stuck around to the very end, I ask that do whatever you can to help others who are job searching. Whether it is by giving feedback, introducing them around the industry, or just being a sympathetic ear, you can make a difference in another's success or ability to cope with the process. Job searching can be tough, but we can make it tolerable if we support one another through each twist and turn.

Thank you for reading,

-Edwin

SHOUTOUTS

Jace the Raccoon
Chapter: 14
-Job hunting is a quest that is easier with support, so talk to every NPC you meet.

Louis Williams
(https://www.writing.com/main/portfolio/view/lu-man)
Chapter: 9
- His first book, *Dreamers of The Sea*, a steamship pirate adventure with foxes, will be published soon on Kindle.

Equine Essayist
(https://www.furaffinity.net/user/equine-essayist/)
Chaptor: 12
- Stories from a stallion.

Brian Renadette
(https://brianrenadette.carrd.co/)
Chapter: 5
-Sometimes known as 'Meck', this rabbit helped create the script for Seasons 2 and 3 of the furry audio drama 'The Adventures of the Fox in the Fedora.

Frances Pauli

(http://francespauli.com)

Chapter: 20

-Award-winning animal fiction for adults.

Tir

(https://www.furaffinity.net/user/tirnanogtir/)

Chapter: 3

-I hope you enjoyed all the short stories in this book, mine included, and I wish you all the best on your path to the job of your dreams!

Packwolf Lupestripe

(https://lupestripe.com/)

Chapter: 4, 6, 19

-Packwolf Lupestripe is a pink and grey husky from the UK, who has had experience of searching for jobs in numerous countries across Europe.

Franklin T. Davis

(furaffinity.net/user/fromthedead)

Chapter: 1, 15, 17

-Just some guy who writes because it's fun.

William Dingo
(@DingoWilliam on X)
Chapter: 7
-This dingo lives in Australia, spectates the sunrise and wags his tail imperceptibly fast when talking about his hobbies like art and writing.

Shiloh Skye
(linktr.ee/shilohskye)
Chapter: 10
-Shiloh Skye is a writer, editor, and lover of furry fiction who can't wait to read your work

Rixor Amsel
(https://linktr.ee/Riksor)
Chapter: 2, 8
-Job hunting is quite the process--remember to take care of yourself! This opossum is rooting for you!

Mel. White
(https://www.furaffinity.net/user/melwhite/)
Chapter: 11, 13, 21
-SFWA member and part of the Furry community since its earliest days, she is mostly known for her comic book work and for her current research work on furry fandom.

* 9 7 9 8 2 1 8 9 8 7 8 4 8 *